THE CORPORATE GOVERNANCE LANDSCAPE OF PAKISTAN

THE CORPORATE GOVERNANCE LANDSCAPE OF PAKISTAN

EDITED BY
SADIA KHAN

FOREWORD BY
ISHRAT HUSAIN

CELEBRATING 70 YEARS OF PAKISTAN
THE PLATINUM SERIES

OXFORD
UNIVERSITY PRESS

OXFORD
UNIVERSITY PRESS

Oxford University Press is a department of the University of Oxford. It furthers the University's objective of excellence in research, scholarship, and education by publishing worldwide. Oxford is a registered trade mark of Oxford University Press in the UK and in certain other countries

Published in Pakistan by
Ameena Saiyid, Oxford University Press
No.38, Sector 15, Korangi Industrial Area,
PO Box 8214, Karachi-74900, Pakistan

First Edition published in 2017

ISBN 978-0-19-940402-5

Typeset in Adobe Caslon Pro
Printed on 80gsm Local Offset Paper

Printed by Sardar Sons Printers, Karachi

Contents

Note from the Editor vii

Note on the Contributors ix

Foreword xiii
Dr Ishrat Husain

Introduction xvii
Khalid Mirza

PART I: Policy Framework: Laying the Foundation of Corporate Governance

Chapter 1 The Genesis of the First Code of Corporate Governance, 2002 3
Ebrahim Sidat

Chapter 2 Revisions of 2012 as a Reflection of the New Mindset 24
Zaffar A. Khan

Chapter 3 Rules for Governance of Public Sector Enterprises 36
Sadia Khan

PART II: Enshrined Principles: Towards Greater Responsibility, Accountability, and Transparency

Chapter 4 Building an Effective and Efficient Board 69
Sadia Khan

Chapter 5 Providing Strategic Leadership 87
Tabish Gauhar

Chapter 6 Focusing on Financial Stewardship and Accountability 106
S. Masoud Ali Naqvi

Chapter 7 Protecting Stakeholders' Rights 160
Dr Parvez Hassan

PART III: Practical Application: Implementing in Letter and Spirit

Chapter 8 Raising the Bar for Director Education 197
Fuad Azim Hashimi

Chapter 9 Assessing the Efficacy of Implementation 206
Arif Masud Mirza

Chapter 10 The Next Act: Women on Boards 220
Sadia Khan

Bibliography 237

Index 239

Note from the Editor

Sadia Khan

The publication provides a comprehensive guide to the existing policy frameworks, principles, and practices of corporate governance prevalent in Pakistan today. It attempts to capture the essence of the corporate environment prevailing in Pakistan on the eve of the introduction of the first Code of Corporate Governance in 2002 and reveals, through subsequent policy additions, the sea change in the mindset that the first set of policy changes facilitated. It is meant both as a historical anthology of work already accomplished under the realm of corporate governance as well as a reference book for future regulators, educators, and practitioners alike.

Part I provides the policy framework that laid the foundation of corporate governance in Pakistan. Through accounts provided by those intimately involved in their crafting, this section explains the rationale behind the introduction of the rules and regulations, the main principles, as well as the enforcement mechanisms used for each type of policy formulation. The first Code of 2002, its subsequent revision a decade later, and the rules for public sector enterprises are all covered in this section.

Part II elucidates the main principles enshrined in these policy formulations. Principles of greater responsibility, accountability, fairness, and transparency are explained in relation to the primary responsibilities of the Board in providing strategic leadership and financial stewardship. This section will act as a ready reference for students of corporate governance and those wishing to enhance their knowledge of Board responsibilities.

Finally, Part III delves into the practical application of the policies and principles, and discusses the requirements of a ready pool of directors and their commitment in ensuring that the implementation of corporate governance is carried out in letter and spirit. It also discusses the results of implementation surveys conducted in 2007 and 2014–15 and what further steps would be required to keep Pakistan on track with international best practices.

This book is in recognition of the fact that a lot of work—some of which remains underappreciated—has already gone into enhancing the corporate governance environment in the country. It is a story told by the pioneers of corporate governance in the country for the benefit of those who will take it to the next level of policy advocacy and enforcement.

Note on the Contributors

Arif Masud Mirza serves as Regional Head of Policy for the Association of Chartered Certified Accountants (ACCA). He leads ACCA's policy agenda across the Middle East, North Africa, and South Asia (MENASA). Prior to this, he was Chief Executive Officer/Head of ACCA Pakistan from 1997 to 2014. In 2012, Arif was nominated by the Securities Exchange Commission of Pakistan (SECP) to join the board of the Institute of Capital Markets, which he served on until 2016. He is also on the editorial board of *Accountancy Futures Journal*. From 1999 to 2004, he was a visiting faculty member at the Lahore University of Management Sciences, teaching advanced accounting electives on the MBA courses and executive courses at the Rausing Executive Centre.

Ebrahim Sidat is a Fellow Member of the Institute of Chartered Accountants of Pakistan (ICAP). He has recently retired as the Country Managing Partner/CEO of Ernst & Young Ford Rhodes Sidat Hyder and Co. (Ernst & Young), Pakistan. He was the Chairman of the Task Force of formulating the first Code of Corporate Governance as well as for the revisions undertaken in 2010.

Fuad Azim Hashimi is a Fellow Member of the Institute of Chartered Accountants in England and Wales and has over forty-five years of experience in public accounting, diversified business and commercial ventures in banking, sales and marketing, information technology, and fund management. He headed the Pakistan Institute of Corporate Governance from September 2007 to August 2016 and is a non-executive Director on the Board of International Industries Ltd, where he is additionally Chairman of the Audit Committee. Mr Hashimi is also a member of the Private Sector Advisory Group of the Global Corporate Governance Forum.

Khalid Mirza, currently Professor of Practice in LUMS, teaches a variety of subjects, including corporate governance. He has fifty years worth of experience, and essentially covers the financial sector in a wide arc: as a securities trader, analyst, portfolio manager, project finance specialist, investment banker, development financier, regulator, adjudicator, and teacher, as well as in the provision of both technical assistance and policy advice. While close to half his career has been with the World Bank Group (primarily IFC), he has also held significant public sector positions, inter alia, Chairman Securities and Exchange Commission (from 2000 to 2003, during which the Code of Corporate Governance was implemented), and Chairman Competition Commission of Pakistan (2007–10).

Masoud Naqvi is a chartered accountant by profession, with experience ranging over forty years of professional practice. He is the former Senior Partner of KPMG Taseer Hadi & Co., Chartered Accountants. He has been the president of a number of professional bodies and institutions, such as ICAP and Management Association of Pakistan. He was a member of ICAP committees for the first Code of Corporate

Governance and subsequently a member of the Review Committee for the Code. Currently, he is the Advisor at KPMG Taseer Hadi & Co. and Chairman of the Tax Reforms Commission of Pakistan.

Parvez Hassan is currently a Senior Advocate, Supreme Court of Pakistan, and Senior Partner, Hassan & Hassan (Advocates). He also serves as a founding and board member of Lahore University of Management Sciences (LUMS), Shaukat Khanum Memorial Trust Hospital, Beaconhouse National University, and Namal College. His prominent affiliations as an environmentalist include Former Chair, World Commission on Environmental Law, International Union for Conservation of Nature, and President, Pakistan Environmental Law Association.

Sadia Khan is a former regulator, educator, and practitioner of corporate governance. Sadia has pursued a versatile career path traversing investment banking, financial regulation, family businesses, and entrepreneurship across three continents. She has been a passionate advocate of corporate governance for the last two decades. While at Asian Development Bank (ADB) in Manila, she helped implement corporate governance reforms in a number of member countries in South East Asia. As a senior member of the Securities & Exchange Commission of Pakistan, she was responsible for the implementation of the first Code of Corporate Governance in Pakistan. Since then, she has served as a member of various Task Forces and Committees responsible for revising the Code and introducing corporate governance guidelines for state-owned enterprises.

As a corporate governance practitioner, she continues to serve on various boards as an independent director. She obtained her B.A (Hons) from Cambridge University, M.A from Yale University, and M.B.A from INSEAD in France. In 2014, the French Government awarded her the prestigious 'Chevalier de l'Ordre National du Mérite' (Knight of the National Order of Merit).

Tabish Gauhar is founder of the emerging market-focused Oasis Energy Consultants and Oasis Power Fund. He served as partner at the Abraaj Group, and as Chairman and CEO of K-Electric between late 2009 and mid 2015.

Zaffar A. Khan graduated as a mechanical engineer. He served Exxon/Engro for thirty-five years, the last six as CEO. Upon retirement, he served as Chairman of PTCL, Karachi Stock Exchange, and PIA. Currently, he is an Adjunct Professor at IBA where he teaches Human Resource Management. He also frequently teaches at the Pakistan Institute of Corporate Governance. Mr Khan has served on a diverse number of Boards in the public and private sectors and civil society organizations. Current Board appointments include Shell Pakistan, International Industries, Privatisation Commission, Askari Bank, Acumen Fund Pakistan, and Pakistan Centre for Philanthropy. Mr Khan has served as the President of the Overseas Chamber of Commerce and Industries and several committees of the Government of Pakistan. Mr Khan is a recipient of the Sitara-e-Imtiaz.

Foreword

Dr Ishrat Husain

Corporate governance has become a buzzword, particularly among those managing and overseeing public listed companies. Some very good initiatives have been taken by the Securities and Exchange Commission (SECP) and State Bank of Pakistan (SBP), such as issuing the Codes of Corporate Governance. Pakistan Institute of Corporate Governance (PICG) has taken a lead in organizing systematic training at regular intervals for Directors of the Boards of various companies. Their example has been followed by many other reputable institutions imparting similar training courses. However, there was a big gap as far as literature on corporate governance in the context of Pakistan was concerned. I am so glad that Sadia Khan, an accomplished practitioner of corporate governance, has taken the initiative in producing this first compilation. I wish to commend her for her hard work in bringing different expert views at one place and filling this gap.

In Pakistan, we have encountered two extremes of accountability as part of corporate governance. Most of the public enterprises are answerable at the same time to their Boards, ministers, parliamentary committees, regulators, Federal Investigation Agency, the National Accountability Bureau, and the Anti-Corruption Bureau. This overkill of accountability has led to paralysis and indecision, thus negating the very purpose for which the mechanism of accountability has been prescribed as an integral part of corporate governance. At the other extreme, we have ritualistic or perfunctory practices of accountability at many companies. Boards and Audit Committees are established to fulfil the requirements of the Code of Corporate Governance. All boxes are ticked as being fully complied with. Board Directors are trained and certified but the composition of the Board is so tilted and the quality of their expertise so weak that fierce accountability is more in name than real. We also do not have activist shareholders, corporate raiders, private equities, and hedge funds eager to acquire undervalued companies that can be turned around with superior management or analysts who dive deeper into the company's financials to unearth inefficiencies or misallocation of capital. In the absence of such external restraining factors, a number of companies continue to show losses in public disclosures while their sponsors enjoy opulent living standards. This is being done under the same sanctified Corporate Governance Code that has been ticked off by the Boards. Transparency, integrity of financial statements, and accountability are all taken for a ride. If that is not enough, of the entire universe of 65,000 companies registered with the SECP, only 550—less than one per cent—are listed on the Karachi Stock Exchange. Theoretically, only this small subset are obliged to comply with the Code of Corporate Governance. The standards and practices of other private and family-owned companies remain shrouded in mystery.

The effects of the transformation of family businesses and unlisted private companies into business houses are quite widespread and can affect economic growth, expansion of employment, efficient allocation, and utilisation of capital and human resource development in a positive way. This would require different listing requirements for medium and small enterprises, flexible and less intrusive rules, and innovative corporate governance standards. The 'one size fits all' approach cannot achieve this. A more diversified and tailor-made approach should be used.

The challenge before all who are interested in spreading the practices of good corporate governance, both in letter and spirit, is to introduce its understanding and awareness, and inculcate a sense of responsibility right from an early stage. For example, all business schools producing future corporate executives for the country should have a course on corporate governance and business ethics as a requirement for their degree. Excesses by private sector managers to perpetuate their own interests can be curbed and the protection of minority shareholders ensured if the oversight and exercise of fiduciary responsibilities by the Board is made effective, prudent, and embedded in the highest ethical standards. The roles and responsibilities of the external auditor and the regulator have to be made more biting. The change, therefore, has to originate in the mindset and values at a young age, when we are trying to shape their personalities and influence their way of thinking. The world around us is full of dilemmas and hard choices. Principles and practices of corporate governance should aid these young men and women in making the right choices. These may put them in difficulties in the short term, but they should rest assured that in the long run they would be better off avoiding temptation and sticking to the right course.

I wish to thank Sadia for this excellent work and hope that she will continue to provide us with materials, case studies, and illustrations of ethical dilemmas faced by corporate executives and real world examples that we can use in our classrooms and seminars.

Introduction

Khalid Mirza

THE CONTOURS OF CORPORATE GOVERNANCE

It is now universally acknowledged as an incontestable proposition that corporations must adhere to sound norms of corporate governance and that the operating environment, as fostered by law, regulation, and codes of practice, must stipulate and encourage compliance with such norms. What does this mean?

CORPORATE GOVERNANCE: THE BASICS

Corporate governance, as suggested by Sir Adrian Cadbury, is the 'system by which companies are directed and controlled'. It differs from management inasmuch as it is not the actual running of a company along with the related decision-making, which is the domain of management, but the system in accordance with which companies are managed, including the necessary monitoring and controls, and the checks and balances seeking to ensure that companies are managed in a robust manner.

A company or a corporation—colloquially often called a 'corporate'—is a creature of law, a legal artifact that not only cannot go beyond the limits imposed by law but is also confined to act within the stipulations contained in its registered foundation documents, i.e. the Memorandum and Articles of Association. There is ample legal precedent regarding its operational scope and what it can and cannot do. Anything done outside these boundaries would be ultra vires and of no legal consequence.

Ordinarily, the shareholders of a company are only liable for the company's obligations to the extent of the capital subscribed and no more. It is noteworthy that on occasion, in the case of 'private' limited companies that have only a few investors (or even a single shareholder), the courts have deemed it fit, for reasons recorded by them, to effectively 'pierce' the corporate veil of limited liability and hold the shareholders (or a specific shareholder) liable for the obligations of the company beyond the subscribed capital. Such an eventuality is unlikely in the case of a 'public' limited company that characteristically has obtained its capital through subscriptions made by a large number of widely distributed shareholders, which is the essence of what a company is and the economic *raison d'être* of its existence. The widely dispersed shareholders of a public company (or indeed institutional shareholders representing a large number of investors) obviously have a keen interest in a sound system which ensures that the company is duly governed and looks after the legitimate interests of all its shareholders and also other stakeholders as may be relevant to the circumstances of the company.

Clearly, an efficacious governing system becomes a necessity when it is not possible or practical for a company's affairs to be managed by all its shareholders, and pragmatically, at least some, if not all, shareholders have to be excluded. It is this fundamental reality that makes an appropriate governance system essential for public companies, especially those listed, in order to impart a sense of confidence to investors in these companies. Conversely, it is for these reasons that corporate governance norms have very little relevance in the case of unlisted private companies, and state-owned (unincorporated) enterprises.

PRINCIPAL-AGENCY CONCEPTUAL UNDERPINNING

As conceived in the Companies Ordinance, 1984 (and in the corporate laws of most common law countries), corporate governance rests on a cascade of principal-agency relationships, namely: the Board of Directors, comprising representatives of the shareholders, is the agent of the shareholders; and the Chief Executive Officer (CEO), appointed by the Board, is the agent of the Board. The CEO then appoints senior executives like the Chief Operating Officer (COO), Chief Financial Officer (CFO), etc., usually with the advice and consent of the Board. These senior executives have their sub-agents, as it were, i.e. other executives working under them as approved by the CEO.

While the principal-agency paradigm runs through the company, the centrepiece of corporate governance is the Board of Directors. The design and composition of the Board—i.e. its functionality and processes—constitutes the kernel of corporate governance. This is important because the Board is the instrument through which the management, led by the CEO, is directed and controlled. Effectively, the monitoring, supervision, and oversight of the CEO (and those executives immediately reporting to the CEO), as well as substantively determining the company's strategic plans in conjunction with the CEO, comprise the primary responsibilities that the Board is expected to discharge both as representative of the shareholders and in compliance with the imperatives enshrined in the company law as well as in the Memorandum and Articles of Association.

As indicated above, the system of corporate governance in Pakistan, and in many other countries, is underpinned by the principal-agency concept. It is designed to reduce agency costs believed to arise from the perception that all economic players are opportunistic and self-serving 'utility maximizers'. Their foremost aim is to somehow seek out and serve their own interest, notwithstanding the inconvenience of any contractual obligations they are expected to fulfil. This proposition is underscored in spades by the chain of checks and balances and other devices built-in to ensure that the contractual obligations constituting the corpus of corporate fundamentals are faithfully discharged by the parties concerned. Obviously, it is in recognition of the need to realize this aim that a web of best governance practices—including stipulations contained within corporate legislation—are duly implemented by corporate players.

OTHER PATTERNS OF CORPORATE GOVERNANCE

The principal-agency based, shareholder-oriented, and shareholder value maximising corporate governance paradigm, embedded in the common law tradition alluded to in the preceding paragraphs—and extant in most of the English-speaking world, as well as in many jurisdictions beyond, sometimes with minor variations—is by no means universal. There are fairly distinct, perhaps even fundamental, deviations from this basis of corporate governance, which subsist in several significant jurisdictions, including those in Western Europe, Latin America, and East Asia. Two of these 'deviant' models of corporate governance are prominent and deserve to be recorded.

First, as opposed to the agency approach, the Chief Executive and senior executives reporting to her/him and other executives down the line are not viewed as 'agents' (with all the suspicions and agency costs this entails) but rather as good stewards in a very trusting approach. It is believed that ordinarily the human response to trust is mostly favourable and positive. The stewardship approach is not supported by any provisions in law, nor does it have any structural basis arising from any code of practice. It is simply more of an attitude that is reflected in the behaviour of corporate players, and can, therefore, manifest itself within the formal principal-agency framework despite its diametrically different philosophical underpinning. Both principal and agent (i.e. the steward in this case) must be genuinely committed to the stewardship approach for the situation to be productive and worthwhile.

A principal that treats the agent as a steward while the latter does not behave as such would clearly be a most untenable state of affairs. It is also obvious that circumstances involving an agent behaving like a steward, but not treated as such by the principal, would be similarly untenable from a governance standpoint. In Pakistan, many large family-owned companies, particularly in the textile sector, seem to have adopted the stewardship model or possibly some kind of quasi-stewardship governance pattern. The stewardship approach is to a great extent in evidence in Japan, to a lesser degree in continental Europe, and sporadically in other countries, including diehard adherents of the principal-agency model like the United States (US) and Britain.

Second—and more importantly—is the 'stakeholder' model of governance that takes a conceptually different view of a corporate from that of the shareholder-oriented, common law-based model whereby unequivocal recognition is given to the fact that the shareholder is the 'owner' and real beneficiary of the activities of a corporation which, in its final analysis, is viewed as a nexus of contracts for the ultimate benefit of the shareholders, i.e. designed to maximize shareholder value. In the stakeholder model, largely in vogue in Germany and Japan—and to a lesser extent in other European countries—the shareholder is viewed as a 'restricted' owner who has a residual economic interest by virtue of the risk capital provided on a limited liability basis but has no further contribution to make. The stakeholder model recognizes the importance and contribution made by a host of stakeholders, both in the community as well as those with whom formal and implied contracts have been concluded, and the corporate is visualized as a web or constellation of several stakeholders, one of whom is the shareholder. It is the value added from relationships with stakeholders that are deemed to have priority over any contributions derived from contracts, including the equity investment contributed. Primacy of the shareholder is not a salient feature of the stakeholder model and jurisdictions adopting this model attach considerable importance to the role played by other stakeholders. Also, in these jurisdictions, it has been empirically observed that in relative terms, corporates exhibit reduced levels of equity, being primarily financed by various categories of debt obligations.

While in a sense corporates constructed and governed in terms of the stakeholder model are believed to be more stable and sustainable, there are obvious questions as to their ability to attract risk capital by way of equity investment. To attract equity subscriptions, it would be necessary to price the shares rationally, keeping in view any amounts extracted, or to be extracted, for the benefit of all other stakeholders. Ordinarily, the stakeholder model entails a large proportion of the company's equity held by a variety of stakeholders (including creditors), which, unlike pure equity investors, have an additional, material, vested interest in the company. Such stakeholders are also substantially represented on the Board (or supervisory Board, in the case of dual Board structures). All this means is that not only would the discipline of the marketplace via hostile takeover bids be difficult to achieve, but also that raising substantial equity amounts via a global IPO would be a challenge unless it is attractively priced.

Although it is easier said than done, a degree of convergence of the shareholder and stakeholder models is possible—at least theoretically. It is clear that without detracting from its purity, the shareholder-oriented model can be modified so as to co-opt within it the spirit of the stakeholder model. Forthcoming and accommodating measures, supportive of major stakeholders aimed at fostering mutually beneficial relationships, can be justified as a sound business proposition on a long-term basis. This is opposed to the short-range perspective inherent in the shareholder-oriented model. Of course, as indicated earlier, adopting the stewardship approach simply entails a change in attitude and behaviour on the part of both principals and agents. Since old habits die hard, this is also easier said than done. Overall, while convergence of the various governance models is in theory quite possible, it is difficult to achieve practically.

ESSENTIAL SCOPE

Whatever the pattern of governance is—whether in its pure form or modified through partial convergence with another model—corporate governance covers three aspects:

i. Composition and role of the Board of Directors as the governing body of the company. This is the centrepiece of corporate governance.
ii. Role of management and instituting, as well as implementing, a system of internal controls to protect the integrity of the corporate. The most significant development in this respect is the Sarbanes-Oxley Act,

2002 (SOX) of the US, a paradigm shift in corporate governance (radical reform of corporate reporting and controls, ensuring reliable audits, management of board responsibilities, etc.).

iii. Protection of minority shareholder interests.

In most jurisdictions, corporate laws together with regulations made thereunder, as well as stock exchange listing rules and codes of corporate practice, amply cover these matters.

Also, in a large number of jurisdictions—including Pakistan—reasonable efforts have been made to cover issues pertaining to internal controls, reliable audits, reporting, etc., covered by (ii) in the preceding paragraph. Apart from globally recognised principles, specific local circumstances are an important factor that need to be given due consideration in order to be efficacious in this respect. And as regards (iii) above, i.e. the protection of minority shareholder interests, this is a vexed question that has been tinkered with partially, and from a variety of angles, but a fully satisfactory answer has remained elusive. On the other hand, the composition and role of the Board of Directors, i.e. (i) above, has received a lot of attention since it is regarded as critical to achieving sound corporate governance; and at least in form and outward manifestation, there appears to be a wide degree of consensus as to the elements of what a single-tier Board should look like and what it should do. Two-tier Boards, à la the German or Dutch stakeholder models, are a different story.

CORPORATE BOARDS—ROLE AND DESIGN

While corporate laws and the relevant codes of practice made applicable to companies in many countries specify the duties and responsibilities corporate Boards are expected to discharge, in general terms, all this means is that a corporate Board is required to monitor and oversee management as well as provide it strategic guidance. However, at a substantive and practical level, it has been often observed that Board members have merely an advisory role to play, and that apart from this, an important function of the Board is to select the CEO whenever there is a vacancy. Despite this somewhat limited de facto functionality, Board members remain fully liable for the stipulated *de jure* responsibilities.

In the wake of recent corporate governance disasters, the received wisdom is that to be effective, a corporate Board must be designed such that it is limited in size (say, not more than ten or eleven directors), of which at least two-thirds should be non-executive directors (NEDs) and such that at least half the NEDs should be 'independent', i.e. without any material interest in the company other than Board directorship. Some governance buffs firmly believe that a majority of the Board should comprise independent directors. It is furthermore felt—as opposed to the American corporate tradition—that the Board should not be chaired by the CEO but rather by one of the independent directors, and if for some reason this is not feasible, the Board must have a 'lead director' elected by the independent directors, and the duty of determining the agenda for Board meetings should be entrusted to either the independent, non-CEO Chairman or the lead director. Here, it is also considered important that the independent directors meet regularly (say, once a quarter), separately and without the CEO or the executive directors to inter alia take stock of the company's affairs. In addition, as part of its working methodology, the Board should possibly have three committees covering the areas of audit, human resource/governance (including responsibility for Board nominations, senior appointments, succession planning, etc.) and compensation, each of which must comprise a majority of independent directors (including the chair of each committee). It is important that the functioning of the Board is essentially in the hands of independent directors/NEDs and not the CEO (though the CEO should be consulted).

It is clearly considered best practice for Boards to approve, after due consideration, the company's strategic direction as well as assess the efficacy of actions taken in this connection. In addition, it is the Board's responsibility to assess the performance of senior management, including the CEO, determine their tenure and compensation, and engage in necessary succession planning. Also, Boards are increasingly required to evaluate their own performance; however, there are questions with respect to the modus operandi on how best to accomplish this goal.

The Board governance scheme outlined above places considerable reliance on independent directors. This is the Achilles heel since an independent director can also very easily be a disinterested director. It is, of course, quite possible to motivate independent directors by including in their compensation package an element aligned to corporate goals/shareholder value enhancement. However, this could detract from true independence via the incentive provided to independent directors to become partial to riskier, higher profit potential projects and schemes, thus promoting short-term enhancements in shareholder value.

It is also clear that the aforementioned scheme of Board governance (regarding which there is a fair degree of consensus) may not necessarily deliver the desired level of Board effectiveness or management performance. Directors are constrained by the time they are able to devote to Board duties and by the level of actual knowledge they have regarding the company's business, as also, very often, by the sector in which the company operates, both in the local context as well as the international.

GUARDING AND FOSTERING CORPORATE GOVERNANCE

Effectively, the scheme of governance as per the shareholder-oriented model (in vogue in Pakistan) relies on several institutional props that serve as 'guards' or 'gatekeepers' to ensure that the Board and management faithfully play their part. Within the Board, the presence of independent directors and the various important Board committees (significantly, the audit and nomination committees) could potentially go a long way towards keeping the Board and management honest, checking any self-serving by executive functionaries, ensuring adherence to overall corporate goals and protecting the interests of the minority. Furthermore, the company's auditors, its creditors (in particular banks and financial institutions), the credit rating agencies, the security analysts and commentators and the stock market (including its capacity to cause hostile takeover bids) constitute an institutional framework, which if not corrupted or perverted or compromised has the capacity to maintain the viability of the system.

Notwithstanding the challenges, it is clear that instituting sound norms of corporate governance is a cornerstone of the efforts to create an environment that is attractive for capital. At a simplistic level, it is also fairly obvious that the essential requirements—and outward manifestation—of sound corporate governance is really fairly basic, almost inane. With the exception of a few onerous requirements recently imposed by law in some advanced jurisdictions, like certain provisions of the US Sarbanes-Oxley Act, corporate governance is like good housekeeping. Why should anyone make a big deal of it? The strong opposition in very nearly all developing countries to even the most basic set of principles of corporate governance is quite astounding. It is noteworthy that the opposition almost invariably comes from all quarters!

Here it must be pointed out that insofar as corporate governance is concerned, most economic managers, development bankers and securities regulators in developing countries find themselves handicapped because the social and commercial pressures to promote good governance just do not exist. In developed countries, these pressures have been known to come from three sources:

- Mutual funds/pension funds, i.e. institutional investors, seeking safeguards for their investments. CALPERS in the US was the progenitor of corporate governance norms and has remained a prominent proponent.

- A strong shareholder movement. In some European countries such movements have forced managements to adhere to due process and other norms of governance.
- Professional activism, which has also been responsible in some countries for promoting improvements in corporate governance, as has happened in Britain where various professional bodies have been active advocates of better governance.

This kind of push for corporate governance is largely absent in developing countries, including those in Asia.

Further, we must remember that a conducive environment for corporate governance essentially comprises four elements:

- A sound value structure, i.e. a high moral plane;
- A basic framework of laws and regulation;
- A judicial system and an enforcement mechanism that actually works; and
- Separation of ownership from management.

Barring a few exceptions here and there, none of these essential elements are present in any substantial sense in most developing countries. A large number of countries both inside and outside Asia do not have more than two of these four elements in place. Hence the ground is not fertile in these countries for corporate governance to develop firm and deep roots. Thus so far in developing Asia, corporate governance is either confined to a few corporates, or is really superficial or not sustainable.

THE BENEFITS

Despite these odds, securities regulators and economic managers have to persevere because not only do jurisdictions that have implemented the accepted norms of governance attract more capital but because these norms are among the cardinal reasons for regulation of the capital market; namely, to ensure that there is due process and all stakeholders get a fair shake. It is immaterial whether or not one follows to the letter any codified set of corporate governance norms. It is, on the other hand, very important to put in place within the circumstances of the enterprise, systems that are transparent, that call for due process, that enhance accountability to shareholders, that provide for adequate parameters to resolve conflict, and that provide for a fair return to all stakeholders. However onerous this may seem, there is no doubt that the enterprise benefits remarkably if it adheres to the principles of good corporate governance by way of overall efficiency and better performance as well as satisfied stakeholders. There is considerable empirical evidence that directly correlates the level of good governance achieved with capital inflows from international institutions, and indirectly with lower cost of capital and higher share values.

A recent survey by an eminent global consulting firm showed institutional investors willing to pay a premium of more than 20 per cent for shares of Asian companies that demonstrate adherence to the norms of good governance. The Asian financial crisis of 1997 was to a lesser or larger degree—depending on how one sees it—caused by a lack of adherence to acceptable governance practices among corporates in general and the financial sector in particular. It is, therefore, necessary to do whatever is needed in order to institute sound corporate governance in Pakistan. Certainly, over the last several years there has been a lot of intellectual ferment in regard to corporate governance, and a number of strong legal and regulatory steps have been taken worldwide to enhance standards of corporate governance and to ensure better implementation of these standards.

FUNDAMENTAL CHALLENGES

There has been a proliferation of carefully devised codes of corporate governance; the OECD principles of corporate governance have been revised to take account of evolving realities, the accounting profession is now under far greater oversight and scrutiny than ever before following the spate of spectacular accounting-related governance scandals that came to light recently, and there is the very potent, and somewhat heavy-handed, Sarbanes-Oxley Act of the US, enacted in response to the recent dot.com and governance fiascos—a law that really constitutes a paradigm shift in corporate governance parameters. It is also noteworthy that various jurisdictions, like the EU, have adopted elements of the Sarbanes-Oxley Act. While it is too early to be definitive, so far there is not much evidence to indicate a change in the wind, and corporate governance failures continue to emerge in different jurisdictions with unacceptable frequency.

The fact of the matter is that corporate governance is a challenging subject. There is no aspect of finance or management that is so difficult to implement in a substantive or genuine sense, whatever the nature and content of the legal and regulatory framework. It seems to be the ultimate in form over substance. While the outward manifestation of a company might reflect full compliance with the best corporate governance norms, this may not in any way represent the true position. When advanced countries suffer from this unsatisfactory state of affairs despite their highly developed traditions, institutions, and sophisticated regulatory enforcement, the situation of most developing countries cannot be better. It could be somewhat worse; albeit empirical evidence to support this contention is not readily available.

Now the question is: why is sound corporate governance so clearly in the interest of corporates and yet so elusive in a substantive sense? The answer lies in the nature of the 'public company': the fact that it necessarily embodies in its functioning the principal-agency relationship, i.e. shareholders with various levels of interest in the company and possibly their own distinct interests being the principals, and management, with or without other interests, being the agent; and the fact is that a company has stakeholders that are both 'insiders' and 'outsiders'. The public company is, as we all know, a juristic person—not a natural person—that has to depend on others to look after its interests. Adam Smith, the father of modern economics, believed that as a concept the public company was doomed to fail since the management of a company did not have any incentive to take care of the interests of widely dispersed shareholders. He would not have been surprised at all by Enron, WorldCom, Tyco, Parmalat, Adelphia, Adecco, and others! He would probably have said: 'I told you so!'

It is interesting to note that most of the spectacular corporate governance failures of the recent past—including some of the ones I just mentioned—had certain common features:

- Firstly, these were very successful businesses.
- Secondly, these companies were in the top, best practice league insofar as implementation of prevalent corporate governance norms was concerned.
- Thirdly, these companies were at the cutting edge with respect to use of technology, financial derivatives, and intricate corporate structures.

All of this suggests that whereas one can appreciate the need for stronger laws and regulations and stronger enforcement—which, indeed, has been the response in most jurisdictions—the real issue for us is whether our corporates have sincerity of intention, the right ethos, and a genuine propensity for good governance.

Also, the governance norms that make most sense, and the implementation modalities that would be best, vary from one jurisdiction to the next based on the prevailing cultural and business environment. For instance, what would make a director 'independent', and indeed how much independent directors can be relied upon, really depends on the local context. It is difficult to imagine what kind of independent directors would be available in a monolithic society with a small, closely-knit business community!

It would be a mistake to simply ape measures that have been adopted in developed countries. In its essence, corporate governance has to relate to local circumstances. The challenge for capital markets regulators is to put in place incentive structures, checks and balances, and other measures so as to elicit a genuine response from corporate managements that ensures the spirit of good corporate governance is duly implemented. The situation of each country is different and measures taken to promote good corporate governance will have to be carefully crafted and customized. Given sincerity of purpose and perseverance, the outcome in most instances should be favourable.

PART I

Policy Framework: Laying the Foundation of Corporate Governance

Chapter 1

The Genesis of the First Code of Corporate Governance, 2002

Ebrahim Sidat

In the context of the corporate world, in the last couple of decades, no subject, in theory or practice, has engaged greater attention of corporate and professional managers, regulators, and academia in most parts of the developed and the developing world than the expression, 'good corporate governance'. Some might wish to argue that it has become a fashionable theme to discuss, write, or talk about. I personally would like to agree with those who ardently believe that without appropriate attention to the fundamental dictates of sound and good corporate governance, it would be difficult, if not impossible, to develop the capital market and grow business enterprises and corporations on a profitable and sustainable basis.

In most jurisdictions, it was witnessed that any formal attempt to enunciate a code of best practices of corporate governance was largely triggered by news headlines dealing with regulatory and other interventions, or probes into major corporate scandals, wrongdoing, and questionable conduct on the part of those charged with governance of corporate and other entities. Once-popular names of players in the corporate sector, particularly in the developed part of the world, have over time become synonymous with corporate misdoings and misdemeanours. Such episodes and events led to the initiation of various measures, including special enactments and formulation of corporate governance regimes relevant to the circumstances of various jurisdictions.

ICAP'S INITIATIVE AND THE PRELIMINARY CHALLENGES

In Pakistan, the accounting profession under the aegis of the Institute of Chartered Accountants of Pakistan (ICAP) took the first groundbreaking initiative when the Fifth All Pakistan Chartered Accountants Conference, usually held once every four years, resolved at Karachi in December 1998 to take the lead for the formulation of an appropriate Code of Corporate Governance (CCG). It was an apt and welcome move by ICAP in the spirit of its contribution and commitment to the promotion and development of the corporate sector in Pakistan along sound and ethical lines. ICAP's decision to launch the CCG project was no less influenced by its belief that proper, transparent and timely corporate reports are inherently an essential concomitant of good corporate behaviour and governance. The accounting profession, by the very nature of its statutory and ethical obligations to the various stakeholders, including investors and the capital market, has a rightful stake in promoting transparency and fairness in the financial reporting chain and communication.

While this underlying objective substantially explained the profession's primary perspective and legitimate interest to take the lead for the task, there was, however, the lingering issue of ownership and enforceability of whatever was expected to emerge or evolve in due course as an acceptable Code. This was, I venture to emphasize, not merely an apprehension, for the profession did hear a few whispers to question obliquely what the accounting profession had to do with the subject of corporate governance and why it should be taking a lead in this task. The sceptics seemed to suggest that the task should be undertaken by the apex regulator—the Securities and Exchange Commission of Pakistan (SECP) or the stock exchanges or such similar bodies. In certain quarters, the questioning of the very need to have for our jurisdiction a separate Code at all and advocating an approach to adopt a Code prevalent elsewhere in other jurisdictions was heard informally. As if this was not enough to dampen the will and zeal of those who volunteered and were sincerely committed to the pursuit of good governance, there were also soundings to the effect that instead of a framework or Code of Corporate Governance, whatever measures for reform are contemplated or appear to be necessary should emanate from and be made part of company law itself. Such and similar observations made here and there, however, did not discourage the profession from proceeding with the task as resolved at the ICAP's Conference with all sincerity and determination of purpose.

THE WAY FORWARD

In order to translate our vision into reality, ICAP constituted a committee comprising past Presidents of ICAP and representatives of the stock exchanges, the Institute of Cost and Management Accountants of Pakistan (ICMAP) and the Chairman of SECP or his nominee.

The Terms of Reference (ToR) of this Committee were determined as follows:

1. To consider and make recommendations for evolving a Code of best practices on the financial aspects, including financial reporting and accountability, in relation to corporate governance in Pakistan.
2. To identify principal issues, having regard to the economic and corporate environment prevailing in Pakistan, impacting:
   a. Interests of various stakeholders in corporate enterprises in Pakistan
   b. Development of healthy and ethical corporate governance practices in Pakistan.
3. To consider and recommend, in the light of the issues identified:
   a. Principles for constitution of an effective Board of Directors:
      - To have due representation of non-executive directors
      - To determine the role and responsibilities of the executive and non-executive directors in relation to financial aspects, reporting and accountability.

b. Need for Audit Committees of the Board, including their composition and role.

4. To consider the 'expectation gap' regarding the role of external auditors, the manner of their appointment, their powers and duties including determination of scope of statutory audit and reporting convention.
5. To consider and identify any other material issue having a bearing on corporate governance in Pakistan.

The ToR also stipulated that the committee will identify the class or type of corporate enterprises in Pakistan to whom the code of best corporate governance practices shall apply and the manner of its enforcement, as also legal or regulatory changes that may consequentially be necessary to implement the recommendations.

The committee was a large and representative group of persons which, at its first few meetings, discussed a few fundamental and preliminary matters relevant to the task and finally decided that for a more focused attention to the subject, a smaller group could best serve the purpose. Hence a sub-committee of five persons was nominated of whom three, being past Presidents of the ICAP, were also members of the main committee, including the author of this Chapter as its Chairman. The fourth member of the sub-committee, representing the Karachi Stock Exchange, was one of its past Presidents and the fifth represented the ICAP's Secretariat as the Member-Secretary. The sub-committee was expected to undertake the tasks pursuant to the above ToR and present its first draft set of recommendations for consideration of the full committee.

PRINCIPLES AND APPROACH ADOPTED IN FRAMING THE CODE

While the subject of corporate governance was not new, as it has been addressed in many countries of the world, both in developed and developing economies, the fact that ours was the first ever institutional effort of its kind in Pakistan distinguished it from other comparable efforts. Our endeavour was further conspicuous by the fact that, while every comprehensive Code arising from the excellent work done elsewhere in the world was available to us, the need to frame a Code responsive to and articulated in the objective circumstances of the Pakistani economy in general, and the complexion and peculiarities of our corporate sector and its culture in particular, needed a tailor-made approach. This naturally meant a huge commitment of time and effort and therefore, right from the inception of the task in April 1999 until the final notification of the CCG 2002 in May 2002 by the SECP, the discussion and deliberations on the subject spanned over thirty formal and intensive meetings, quite a few seminars, and occasional interactions with various groups of stakeholders.

The world has witnessed a major stride forward and an ever-growing interest in good corporate governance but the need to have a Code to address our objective circumstances was increasingly felt as an imperative, which is demonstrated by all the players in the corporate sector; including investors, the financial services community, corporate and banking regulators, and the accounting profession. The committee was therefore faced with the stupendous task of fulfilling the compelling need for a governance framework that is realistic in approach and effective in enforcement. For this to happen, the committee deemed it appropriate to attempt to visualize what is sought to be achieved as the primary objective of our endeavour.

The committee started off with the belief that the corporate governance framework should aim to establish a system or a regime whereby a company is enabled to be directed and controlled by directors having due regard to compliance with the best practices to be enunciated by the Code for carrying out the conduct and affairs of a company. Before the enunciation of the Code, this objective was partly being achieved, and continues to be achieved even now, by the statutory framework in place, i.e. through the main legislation on Company Law matters and quasi-legal and regulatory provisions stipulated by the SECP. The thrust of the Code, however, was aimed at safeguarding by various measures and best practices the interests of diversified stakeholders so as to ensure that the duties and responsibilities of those having a primary and significant say in the affairs of a company are discharged with a sense of propriety, fairness, and transparency, and subject to the desired degree of accountability.

In the context of Pakistan in particular, the need for good corporate governance assumes a more significant dimension given the corporate culture and the overwhelming number of companies which are 'closely' held. The need for a reasonable representation in the corporate decision making process for those not belonging to the controlling interest thus assumes a striking and crucial significance in Pakistan. Accordingly, the Code expects that the Board of Directors should aim to have appropriate representation of minority interest through non-executive, and preferably non-executive independent, directors to discharge their fiduciary responsibilities in the larger interest of all the stakeholders in a transparent, informed, diligent, and timely manner.

In the formulation of the Code, the committee has been conscious of the dictates of corporate democracy enshrined in corporate jurisprudence and recognized over the years, which has not only been substantially preserved but also given due recognition in the Code while seeking to balance it with the inevitable need to safeguard all relevant interests from perceived or potential abuses of corporate power.

The committee has further endeavoured to strike a reasonably acceptable balance to achieve the objectives of good corporate governance by including provisions in the Code to strengthen corporate working and internal controls without seeking in any way to stifle entrepreneurship and sense of business judgment and without creating any hindrance for the forces of competition to have a level playing field. It must, however, be realized that while good corporate governance does play a crucial role in infusing a sense of responsibility and accountability, no such set of measures can absolutely and conclusively prevent all corporate irregularities and malpractices known or perceived to exist in any corporate environment.

The profitability and growth of a business or a corporate enterprise and its sustainability is essentially a function of sound business acumen and judgment to be exercised through strategic direction and prudent policies and strategies to be formulated by the Board of Directors for execution by corporate management, for which a single set of prescriptions is neither feasible nor desirable from a Code's perspective. What, however, the Code may help to achieve is to subject such corporate control and decision-making processes to a more formal and effective degree of discipline and diligence on the part of those in whom the stakeholders have vested their affairs by reposing their trust and confidence. Inevitably, therefore, the principal objective of the Code is to persuade corporate managements to migrate from informal to formal conduct in the affairs of the company with greater attention and due care than earlier observed in dealing with the affairs of a company in the larger interest of all the stakeholders.

In pursuance of the above principles and approach, the committee extensively studied the corporate governance landscape as depicted by the relevant Codes in various jurisdictions. Accordingly, the committee equipped itself with a wealth of knowledge and information from the various Codes enjoying eminent position on the subject, and has benefited immensely from the monumental work done on the subject, including the following:

- The Cadbury Committee Report, UK
- The Greenbury Study Group Report, UK
- The Hampell Committee Report, UK
- The King's Report, South Africa
- The Report on Corporate Governance in Netherlands
- The OECD Principles
- Report of the Hong Kong Society of Accountants
- Recommendations on the Code of Best Practices of corporate governance in Sri Lanka

- Report of Confederation of Indian Industry
- Corporate Governance Practices in Australia
- IFAC's Code of ethics for professional accountants.

An extremely important aspect related to the task was to determine whether the Code to be evolved would simply be expressed in terms of certain cardinal principles on various principal aspects of corporate governance or whether we would go on to formulate a regime of rigid rules on the subject. This necessarily entailed a thorough analysis of the legal framework in Pakistan within which the corporates generally operate, our legal and judicial system, our corporate regulatory mechanism and its capacity and experience to regulate our corporate sector, and various other aspects having implications for the matter. After extensive deliberations, there was consensus on the fact that each of the two approaches of formulating a Code, i.e. principles-based or rules-based has its own merits, but what needed to be assessed and determined is what approach would best work for us in Pakistan, particularly given the fact that a major step forward was being taken in Pakistan in the realm of corporate governance and behaviour and it would therefore be prudent to act with great caution. While the principles-based approach works best and is of greater enduring nature even with changing circumstances, this approach needs, as a condition precedent, strong adherence to laws and respect for best practices, customs, and traditions further augmented by a prompt and competent legal and judicial environment. As opposed to this, the rules-based approach would be preferred in a situation where compliance, enforcement and the economic and corporate environment leave a lot to be desired. On balance, therefore, the ultimate conclusion was that our Code will be based on a hybrid mode, enunciating only principles where deemed appropriate in our circumstances and couched in terms of the specific rules where voluntary compliance in the light of the principles would only potentially result in tardy compliance and lax enforcement.

Preliminary Identification of Principal Issues of Corporate Governance in Pakistan

After intensive deliberations, the committee enumerated the following as the major issues relevant to corporate governance in Pakistan:

1. The Composition of the Board of Directors:
   - Dominance by one or a group of shareholders
   - Sponsor or family members of the promoter generally serving as executive directors, thus obliterating the distinction between ownership, governance and management
   - Weak or total absence of minority shareholders' representation
   - Ineffective role of institutional directors (including non-executive directors, where present)
   - CEO lacks certain fundamental attributes of office and his independence is often impaired
   - Absence of eligibility criteria relating to appointment or nomination of directors

- Limit on maximum number of directorships
- Advisability or otherwise of minimum or maximum age limit
- Qualification requirements

2. Role, Duties, and Obligation of Directors:
   - Management override of controls
   - Nominal or ineffective role of the Board of Directors
   - Abuse of fiduciary powers
   - Conflict of interest, particularly in 'related party' matters and transactions
   - Informal decision-making process leading to a lack of adequate and timely disclosure
   - Attitude of disregard towards the minority interests resulting in a lack of distinction between corporate and private interests
   - Substantial disregard of fiscal obligations to the state and public interest obligations
   - Failure to truthfully disclose the financial affairs of the company
   - Lack of training of directors in terms of their proper statutory and moral obligations
   - Failure to disclose or inadequate disclosure of directors' interests
   - Indifference of directors towards their obligations to formulate and institute proper policies, systems and procedures
3. Directors' Remuneration:
   - Lack of an objective and formal process for determination and approval of remuneration of directors

- Vague disclosure or failure to disclose completely and accurately remuneration, perquisites and benefits of directors

4. Corporate Ownership Structure:
   - Companies generally 'closely' held and do not have broad based corporate ownership
   - Absence of institutional forum to represent minority shareholders' interest
   - Indifference and apathy on the part of minority shareholders in company affairs
5. Auditors:
   - Lack of appreciation of the role of auditor:
   - Verification of hundred per cent transactions
   - Wrong perception of responsibility to detect frauds, errors, illegal acts as the primary objective of audit
   - Misconceived perception of auditors as guarantors of corporate solvency
   - Perceived to be responsible for the preparation of the financial statements
   - No appreciation of the primary and inherent limitations of a statutory audit
   - Lack of adequate skills and training in certain cases
   - Excessive reliance on audit trainees with little supervision
   - Lack of the desired degree of accountability and ineffective monitoring
   - Integrity issues, although not pervasive
   - Users' perception of value-addition by audit versus audit cost

- Ambiguity in reporting exceptions or modified audit reports
- Issues of auditors' independence and objectivity due to:
  - Perceived loyalty to management versus shareholders' competitive pressure;
  - Non-audit work;
  - Should scope of statutory audit be revisited or expanded;
  - Absence of objective criteria for selection and appointment of auditors

6. Other Issues:
   - Ineffective regulatory monitoring and protracted judicial process
   - Skill and capacity issues of regulator
   - Potential abuse of discretionary powers of regulator
   - Compliance with formalities more in form than substance
   - Regulatory regime more extensive than reasonably necessary
   - Ad hoc changes and inconsistencies in government policies and laws affecting corporate sector
   - Divestiture of shares held by controlling interest at real value not otherwise publicly known, to the detriment of minority shareholders

Dissemination of the First Draft of the CCG

After due process of deliberations, the first draft of the CCG surfaced in March 2000, which was contemplated to apply to all listed companies, Unit Trusts, Asset Management Companies, Development Finance Institutions (DFIs), Non-banking Finance Institutions (including *Modarabas* and Leasing companies), banks, insurance companies, corporations, and undertakings in which the federal or provincial governments directly or indirectly own or hold a majority of shares or have a controlling interest. We were conscious of the fact that our recommended ambit of application of the CCG was perhaps over-reaching, particularly given the ground reality that this was the first ever major undertaking of the kind on the subject. Implicit in our approach, however, was to send out in the process of dissemination the well-intended signal that over a period of time, these are the kind of entities that should be made subject to observance of whatever the final shape of things that may emerge in the form of a Code.

Right from the beginning of the task, we were mindful of the fact that it is imperative to have the necessary buy-in from the stakeholders and concerned quarters, and therefore their input and necessary participation in the process of formulation in a meaningful way was indeed essential. Accordingly, the first draft was very widely circulated to over sixty trade bodies, associations and institutions, besides many individuals who were in their own right considered to be knowledgeable on the subject. The list included all the three stock exchanges in the country, Overseas Investors Chamber of Commerce and Industry, Federation of Pakistan Chambers of Commerce and Industry, Management Association of Pakistan, State Bank of Pakistan, Pakistan Bankers' Association, Insurance Association of Pakistan, Leasing Association of Pakistan,

Modaraba Association of Pakistan, Mutual Fund Association of Pakistan, National Investment (Unit) Trust, Karachi Chamber of Commerce and Industry, Lahore Chamber of Commerce and Industry, All Pakistan Textile Mills Association, SITE Association, KITE Association, besides certain academics, leading professional firms and the Institute of Cost and Management Accountants of Pakistan.

It was a gratifying experience to note that the response to the draft was highly satisfactory and the input provided to us was very useful in terms of some new and innovative perspectives. After extensive deliberations on the feedback received, the draft was suitably modified and presented as the Revised Draft of the CCG in May 2000 to the committee. A presentation was given in August 2000 to the SECP on the Second Revised Draft after incorporating changes deemed necessary in the light of the committee's deliberations. Our discussions with the SECP provided thoughtful insight to enable us to further modify the draft and fine-tune the same, which was later circulated to the members of ICAP for their comments and observations. Over the next six months or so, seminars were held at Karachi, Lahore and Islamabad under the auspices of the Management Association of Pakistan, Overseas Investors Chamber of Commerce and Industry and the ICAP, which provided an open forum and a constructive debate on the various provisions of the draft Code was made possible.

I must venture to add at this stage that all suggestions and observations mooted at the various seminars and discussions with various institutional bodies were very helpful and demonstrated open and due process of deliberations throughout the task of formulating the Code. I believe that this was a participative approach, which facilitated a great deal in creating a sense of ownership for the corporate sector and the various stakeholders. During this entire process, a vigorous discussion ensued and the final draft of the CCG 2002 was submitted by us to the SECP in January 2002. After final vetting and publication of the draft, the SECP notified the final version of the CCG 2002 in March 2002. Accordingly, a direction was issued to all the three stock exchanges of the country to enforce the same by incorporating the Code in their respective Listing Regulations.

AN OVERVIEW AND ASSESSMENT OF THE CCG 2002 AS NOTIFIED

It was heartening to note that a long drawn project of enunciating the first ever Code of Corporate Governance in Pakistan reached its final culmination after almost four years of toil and effort in the form of the CCG 2002. It was a sensible decision to make the Code applicable only to the listed companies in Pakistan to begin with, although the State Bank of Pakistan, for valid reasons, notified in June 2002 that the Code shall also be applicable to the branches of foreign banks operating in Pakistan to the extent the same may be relevant and feasible in their circumstances. This was a major and constructive move forward as the whole of the banking system was brought within the ambit of the CCG 2002 besides all the listed companies in Pakistan. The foundation was thus laid for the edifice of good corporate governance in Pakistan, which provided a solid basis for further development and reinforcement of the best practices of corporate governance in the form of the Revised Code of 2012.

There is almost a global unanimity of professional opinion that the Board of Directors is the core of corporate governance, and being the keeper of the corporate conscience, it is the Board that will determine the standard and quality of corporate governance and observance of best practices in any corporate enterprise. It is, therefore, obvious that at all stages of formulation of the Code, considerable time and effort was spent and constructive debate and criticism was witnessed at all group discussions and seminars held in the exposure process.

In articulating our recommended provisions dealing with the Board of Directors, its composition, and the independent element that should be the hallmark of a living, independent and effective Board, we were conscious, having regard to our local conditions and scarce availability of good director resources, neither to make the provisions very rigorous nor render the Boards so ineffective as to turn them into a farce. Evidently, therefore, the provisions of CCG 2002 were a major stride forward in governance whereby reasonable curbs were put on the maximum number of executive directors and provision was made to encourage the Board to have at least one non-executive independent director. This provision inter alia paved the way for further strengthening of the provisions when the Code was revised in 2012, making it compulsory to have at least one and preferably one-third of the total members of the Board as 'Independent Directors'. It is my humble experience that over time there has been considerable progress in improving the quality of a large number of Boards and strengthening the role of the directors in discharge of their governance mandate. However, I do admit to an extent that there is room to argue that the element of independent stewardship is discerned only in letter and not truly in spirit. I, for one, would like to surmise that this is essentially a function of time and there is little need to further stifle the Boards with more exacting provisions of good corporate governance in so far as their composition is concerned.

Without dwelling on the details of various provisions of the Code, it may be pertinent to add that the first CCG 2002 did bring in reasonably effective measures to deal with avoidance of directors' conflict of interest and their disclosure, particularly dealing with the 'related party' transactions and arrangements, maximum number of directorships one can hold at any time, the role, powers and obligations of directors, more effective Board meetings by obliging the Board to mandatorily consider and decide on certain principal issues and matters of significance, the Chairman of the Board encouraged to be preferably a non-executive director, timely disclosures of financial and other material information, and a host of other provisions to bring in corporate discipline and promote good corporate behaviour.

In addition to the above, the mandatory requirement for listed companies to have Audit Committees was introduced in the CCG 2002 with a view to strengthening the Boards in discharge of their financial obligations. Accordingly, the requirement to have a majority of the members of the Audit Committee from amongst the non-executive directors has, in my view, played a major role in improving the financial reporting process and communication.

In order to further fortify the role of external auditors, CCG 2002 made provisions to infuse a greater degree of independence by prohibiting a number of non-audit services that an auditor is not authorized to render to his audit client. By the requirement of engaging Audit Committees in the matter of appointment and remuneration of auditors, the oft-repeated perception about auditors serving at the pleasure of management may have been mitigated to a great extent.

CONCLUSION

One must not lose sight of the fact that the CCG 2002, like any other human formulation, is not and cannot be a perfect or complete Code for all times to come. I, therefore, feel inclined to view it as a pioneering best human endeavour made with all sincerity of purpose on the part of everyone who has played any role in its formulation, and I personally feel indebted to them. The fact that the Code has seen the light of day despite fairly strong resistance from certain quarters speaks volumes about the outcome and success of the endeavour. Guided by my professional experience of public practice for over forty years, I venture to say with little risk of contradiction that the least, in my view, that the CCG 2002 has successfully achieved is to oblige Board members to take their statutory and moral responsibilities seriously. This view I wish to hold in the context of the fact that with the advent of the CCG 2002, the Boards often pause to reflect whether their proposed deeds, decisions and actions are consistent with the legal and ethical norms of good and acceptable corporate behaviour. Time has shown that having provided the pioneering framework through CCG 2002, it became possible after about a decade of working thereof in 2012 to conduct a review of what was desirable and in order. The Code of 2012 is indeed a quantum leap forward in many respects by further strengthening the norms of good corporate governance. In my humble view, the introduction of the CCG 2002 and its advanced version, i.e. CCG 2012, would be held in the history of the corporate sector and its regulation in Pakistan as one of the most serious and significant measures for the promotion of the corporate sector and the safeguarding of the interests of all concerned stakeholders. I leave it for posterity to judge!

Chapter 2

Revisions of 2012 as a Reflection of the New Mindset

Zaffar A. Khan

Pakistan got its first version of the Code of Corporate Governance in 2002. It was introduced by the dynamic, result-oriented SECP Chairman Khalid Mirza. Status quo lovers were not amused, but then it was not easy to get him to change once he had made up his mind. Soon after the Code was in place, it won acceptance, though the quality of implementation was mixed. There was superficial compliance in several cases but there were also many who complied with the spirit of the code. In any case, it was a very good beginning and Pakistan was in the forefront among emerging markets. I personally attended regional networking forums in the Maldives, Amman, and Colombo where we as Pakistan stood out for what had been achieved on this front. In my view, the Code strengthened the functioning of Boards in Pakistan, as many a director became much more aware of his or her role and consequently felt more empowered.

The Code adopted in 2002 involved some of our very eminent Chartered Accountants who played a significant role in drafting the Code. I do recall some consultation taking place with the business chambers but most of the concerns or reservations raised were set aside as SECP at the time was determined to introduce the Code to benefit our capital market and corporate Pakistan.

As the years rolled by, 'good corporate governance' became more and more part of the conversation in Pakistan. Globally as well, there were new initiatives, spurred in part by some high profile corporate failures. Countries that already had Codes strengthened them, whereas other lesser developed economies enunciated their first set of guidelines. An important development in Pakistan was the setting up of the Pakistan Institute of Corporate Governance (PICG). Inspired by SECP, this institute since its inception in 2006 has played an important role in the education and promotion of good corporate governance practices. In 2012, after a decade of experience with the 2002 Code, SECP introduced the revised Code that built on the first version of the Code. This time, PICG was trusted to develop the new Code. PICG put together a task team of professionals with diversified backgrounds, which included the stalwart Chartered Accountants who were involved with the development of the first Code. In fact, the task team was led very ably by one of them, Mr Ebrahim Sidat.

Before dwelling on the development of the 2012 Code, let us briefly take stock of what was achieved with the implementation of the 2002 Code. In my view, for many a company the Board acquired a new existence or a new character. It did not happen overnight, but gradually the Board's narrative changed. The scope or content of meetings' agenda, the level of debate, the quality of disclosures and the overall discipline of meetings all moved up several notches. The best visible indicator of these changes can be seen in the annual and quarterly reports that companies are putting out. If you were to compare the reports being published in the 1990s with those of today, you will note the difference is very pronounced. The requirement of quarterly financial reports, adherence to disclosure guidelines and the overall presentation of the business has made these reports timely, informative and user-friendly. Inside the Boardrooms, there was a greater awareness among directors of their role and responsibility, which enriched Board deliberations. So as not to overstate the case, whilst there was notable progress, there were pockets of apathy and cynicism and also some sponsor directors who were not so keen to share their decision-making authority with the Board.

In the case of Pakistan, all our listed corporate entities have predominant shareholders or sponsors, i.e. holding much more than 50 per cent of the equity of the enterprise. This is true for multinationals, family owned, or state-owned enterprises. This is distinct from many of the developed economies where shareholding is much more dispersed and/or is held by institutions such as pension funds, etc. The challenge in companies with predominant shareholders is the desire of the predominant shareholder to call the shots or have things their way, which can undermine the interests of other stakeholders. In cases where the sponsors are enlightened, even though they have the voting power to push through decisions, they make a genuine effort to explain their viewpoint and ensure they are not contravening any law or the principles of fair play. However, as we know, not all sponsors are enlightened and in effect end up harming investor confidence and the capital market. The underlying design of the Code was and is to make it difficult for such forces to prevail. Through a process of awareness building, articulating the benefits of recommended Board practices and specific check measures, there have emerged visible signs of progress and maturity in the corporate world. We have been blessed with a robust stock market, which in part is attributable to improved corporate governance practices.

A decade is a reasonable period of time to review and take stock of the impact of any policy initiative, in this case the introduction of the 2002 Code of Corporate Governance. Whereas many of the beneficial features were becoming apparent, there were areas being talked about that could bring about further improvements. Alongside, we had the world as our workshop to learn and benefit from. Based on lessons from global corporate failures and dedicated research findings, most countries reviewed their governance standards and made changes to up the bar on good practices. A notable example here is the Revised Code of the UK, which is a very comprehensive and extremely well written document. It had special appeal or relevance also because our own company law and norms of company structure and work practices have their roots in the UK system.

To take the next step in the development of the Code, PICG in consultation with SECP put together a 12-member task force in December 2007. The mandate for the task force was to review the existing Code and recommend changes that would further enhance good corporate governance in Pakistan. The team met 22 times and approached the task by reviewing the 2002 Code clause by clause. The task team had a few members who had framed the first Code and so could provide the rationale that prevailed at that time. The team had many more new members who challenged some of the earlier assumptions and provided fresh insights. The debate necessitated review of other global codes as well as identifying best practices that could be applied to our local situation. Through this process the task force evolved its recommendations and then held wider stakeholder consultations in Karachi, Lahore, and Islamabad. The recommendations thus evolved were forwarded to the SECP for adoption. Not all the recommendations were accepted as the SECP decided to undertake another round of consultations under its own supervision where a few of the task force recommendations were modified to accommodate the viewpoint of the participants of these round table consultations. Looking back, the task force found the 2002 Code was well put together and substantially relevant in 2012 as well. However, about a dozen new recommendations were proposed and finally incorporated with some modifications into the new 2012 Code. The SECP Chairman this time was Mr Muhammad Ali. He took a keen interest, was a consensus builder, and was fortunately also decisive in the end.

A BRIEF SYNOPSIS OF THE KEY CHANGES IN THE NEW CODE, TOGETHER WITH THE RATIONALE

Board Composition

The first area of focus was the composition of the Board of Directors (BoD). It was recognized that the BoD has by far the most influence on corporate governance standards of any entity. A balanced Board was viewed as an essential feature for this to happen. Having more independent directors and fewer executive directors would improve the balance and allow for a more robust debate and wider coverage of issues and opportunities in Board meetings. It was therefore proposed that not less than one-third of the Board directors should be independent and no more than one-third should be executive directors. The recommendation of independent directors was vehemently opposed by some in the stakeholder consultations as it was felt to be an infringement on the right of the majority shareholders to run their enterprise according to their wishes and vision. Some said the independent director had no skin in the game, some felt there were not enough suitable independent directors available, etc. The fact that the majority shareholder has a say in the selection and subsequent election of the independent director did not impress. The SECP eventually decided to make having one independent director on the BoD mandatory but with a statement to encourage having one-third of the BoD as independent.

Limiting Executive Directors to a maximum of one-third was more readily accepted. The rationale for this is to create more room for external perspectives at the Board to be introduced. The know-how and perspectives of Executive Directors can in any case be tapped by the Board without offering them a seat on the Board. It is also my experience that in Board meetings, Executive Directors seldom challenge the viewpoint of the CEO or the Chairman of the Board.

Defining Independent Director

The benefit of having independent directors on the Board can only be achieved if the persons inducted under this head are truly independent. To strengthen that outcome, the criterion for assessment of independence was substantially strengthened. A person having any personal interest in the company's business, and its sponsors and key management staff are not eligible. Relationships that get cultivated over time also now debar a person being labelled independent. To persons who say independent directors have no skin in the game, I say get honourable professionals and you can be assured that they will stand up for merit and fair play to further the interests of the corporation.

Separation of Chairman and CEO Positions

Another important change incorporated is that the same person cannot be both Chairman and CEO of the company at the same time. Across the globe, this provision has been debated as arguments for and against segregation of the positions are offered. Increasingly though, it is being held that when the positions are combined, a 'conflict of interest' situation arises. For example, the Board is expected to hold management accountable and this becomes awkward, if not difficult, if the leader of management and leader of the Board are the same individual. I have personally had the opportunity to serve as CEO, Chairman of the Board, and Chairman-cum-CEO of major corporations of Pakistan and can say from my experience that the CEO and Chairman are two distinct positions and should be held by separate persons in the best interests of the corporation.

Human Resource and Remuneration Committee

A major new provision included in the Code requires the Board to constitute a Human Resource and Remuneration Committee. The justification for this committee is to get the Board to consciously engage with arguably the most valuable asset of any corporation—its people. Thus, aside from the requirement in the 2002 Code to have a Board Audit Committee for oversight of the material and financial assets of the company, it is now mandatory to have this second committee covering the human assets. A lot of debate took place on the formation of this committee. There was a fear that this would allow the Board to interfere in management functions, create overlaps and, more bluntly stated, trigger turf wars. Here again, guidelines have been provided to keep the role of the Board at the policy level and limiting individual coverage to the CEO and to some extent to his direct reports. I have had the opportunity to serve on the HR Committee of several organizations and can say with confidence that the committee helped in strengthening the organization. The best example I can offer to illustrate the point is that of Engro. What Engro has been able to achieve is in great measure attributable to the focus it places on managing its human talent. The HR Committee of the Board is an integral part of this area of emphasis.

Number of Directorships

It was the view of the task force that the provision that allows a person to hold up to 10 directorships of listed companies was excessive and reduces the effectiveness of such persons to fulfil the entrusted responsibility. This in part is also because Board meetings tend to be held in narrow windows, which makes it difficult to physically attend all the meetings. The task force recommended a limit of five listed company Boards but this was increased to seven by the SECP following the feedback received in the stakeholder consultation. The increasing accountability and expectations from Boards suggests that directors must ensure they can give enough time to fulfil their responsibilities. Invariably, if you are on a Board, you get to be on a committee of the Board as well. Besides, directors often have other engagements as well on, say, Boards of non-listed companies, NGOs, etc. My view is that five directorships of listed companies are plenty and should eventually be the limit.

Board Evaluation

While the new Code has attempted to further strengthen the Board, it was also keen to strengthen the accountability of the Board. A step in that direction is to require the Board to formally evaluate its own performance once a year so that it takes steps to improve its own performance. The Board is required to disclose to its shareholders in the annual report that it has undertaken the self-evaluation exercise. Very few companies in Pakistan were doing this, including the otherwise progressive companies. Now that it is mandatory, it is to be seen if the Boards limit evaluation to just the Board as a whole or will go the extra mile to evaluate each director. I for one would encourage Boards to undertake individual Director Evaluation including the Chairman of the Board. Boards should find ways to undertake this exercise without politicizing the Board. If done well, it should enhance the efficiency of the Board and add value to the enterprise.

Other Changes

Aside from the above, a few other changes were incorporated, such as director training under any recognized programme, appointment/termination and terms of employment for CFO, Company Secretary, and Head of Internal Audit (IA), qualification required for IA, outsourcing of IA functions, and remuneration of directors. The details on all these can be referenced in the Code document. All these changes are motivated by the desire to create checks and balances by dispersing power from individuals to the Board and providing greater job security to some critical positions in the company. In Pakistan, we often say that there are plenty of laws on the statute books but the problem is in the enforcement. So the question arises whether the Code will meet the same fate. SECP has made the three stock exchanges the enforcement arm whilst keeping oversight with itself. The exchanges have done a decent job of enforcement. Non-compliance can lead to delisting, but before that there are other corrective steps such as letters of warning, imposing fines and ultimately delisting. A key strategy to strengthen compliance is the requirement for Board directors to undergo training in Corporate Governance leading to certification. PICG has played a pioneering role in building this capacity and today other institutions such as ICAP are also offering certification programmes. The best enforcement has to come from within the Board itself; however, the shareholders have to play their part as well. The law provides shareholders the opportunity to question Boards at the Annual General Meetings and they also have a say when electing directors. Using the standards specified in the Code, shareholders can and should be more demanding in holding Boards accountable for compliance with all provisions of the Code.

I first came on a Board as a director in late 1982. Since then, I have served on the Boards of well over 20 entities. These include some of Pakistan's premier institutions, both in the private and public sectors. Over all these years, I have observed an appreciable change in the dynamics of Board meetings. All types of companies have undergone change—some more than others. Sponsors who set up Boards with the sole objective of keeping control end up with rubber-stamp Boards. This may reduce the challenge sponsors face, but in the long run is often detrimental to the well-being of their company. Such Boards miss out on examining new diverse ideas, having quality debates, and undertaking institution building strategies.

An important new sector is the emerging Civil Society Organizations (CSOs/NGOs) who are playing an increasingly important role in the development of the country. The CSOs and fully owned government entities, though not listed and thus exempt from the provisions of the Code, can only benefit if they recognize the spirit of the Code and voluntarily adopt it. It is hoped and expected that the new Code will push the standards of corporate governance in our listed corporations to new improved levels, which in turn will benefit the company and all its stakeholders. Further, it is hoped that the standards applicable in the listed companies will be role modelled or emulated by our non-listed companies and CSOs. Good governance will be the key to our success and well-being as a country. The corporate sector has made progress but more needs to be done.

Chapter 3

Rules for Governance of Public Sector Enterprises

Sadia Khan

INTRODUCTION

The *raisons d'être* for public sector enterprises (PSEs) in any economy are two-fold: to provide services that cannot be equitably provided by the private sector or to protect strategic interests that cannot be managed effectively under private ownership. In some economies, certain enterprises are kept under state ownership for purely investment purposes, so that their profits contribute in a meaningful way to the country's coffers.

In Pakistan, there are currently about 220 PSEs, which fall under some form of partial or full state ownership. There is, however, a need to rationalize this list in the interest of segregating them as strategically important or of investor interest.

The performance of PSEs has come under public debate due to their lacklustre performance over a period of time. A number of PSEs have been incurring losses and have become the so-called 'white elephants of Pakistan's economy'.

Realizing the impact of the governance structure on the inept performance of the PSEs in Pakistan, a task force was constituted by the government to propose new guidelines for the governance of PSEs. This paper discusses the salient features of these guidelines and proposes the implementation strategy in the light of international experiences.

For the purposes of this study, an in-depth analysis of notable and exemplary PSE structures in the world has been undertaken. OESC, Singapore, Malaysia, New Zealand, Finland, and India and their respective experiences have been kept as yardsticks and benchmarks for our recommendations.

Public sector losses are one of the major factors impeding growth. According to some estimates, the poor performance of PSEs in Pakistan results in an estimated loss of almost 1.5 per cent of GDP due to inappropriate governance, corruption, inefficiencies and lapses in policy making.

This is a grave situation that calls for urgent action. Considering the severity of the matter, it is imperative for PSEs in Pakistan to have a code of governance that helps them in uplifting their performance through transparency, accountability, and integrity. The following sections discuss the necessity of a separate Code of Corporate Governance for PSEs in Pakistan, and how to make it more meaningful and result oriented in the light of international practices, norms, and implementation methodologies.

RATIONALE

The government does not have any consolidated data or

central management information system that could offer a comprehensive perspective on the operational and financial performance of PSEs in Pakistan. Similarly, ownership and oversight is dispersed and fragmented, being with sector ministries who do not have a transparent policy framework or reporting on PSEs under their domain. This has had a negative impact on the quality of oversight as the ministries often lack the capacity and understanding of the principles of governing state enterprises. Limited recognition of the need for safeguarding public assets and enhancing their market valuation by the concerned ministries have led to pervasive state interference in PSE affairs and appointments, over-employment and skill mismatches. These interventions of the ministries into the operational affairs of the PSEs have opened the doors to corruption and conflicts of interest within the PSEs, resulting in huge losses to the exchequer. Some specific examples of under par performance of PSEs in Pakistan are as follows.

Pakistan International Airlines (PIA)

- As of January 2016, PIA's cumulative losses are estimated to be over PKR255 billion and liabilities at PKR320 billion. Over and above this, the government has offered long term financing to PIAC for working capital management, guaranteed its borrowing and paid financial charges on selected debt securities.
- Punctuality declined and reached 72 per cent at end 2014 compared to 81.5 per cent in 2007.

- PIA has the highest number of workers per working aircraft. This reached over 700 employees per aircraft in 2015 compared to a global average of 150–200 employees per aircraft.

Pakistan Steel Mills (PSM)

- As of end 2015, PSM's accumulated losses and liabilities, which stood at PKR26 billion at end 2008, had increased to about PKR350 billion, including PKR160 billion in losses and PKR190 billion in payable debt liabilities.
- The government has injected over PKR85 billion out of the federal budget in different bailout packages.
- By January 2015, PSM had achieved only 16 per cent capacity utilization against a target of 77 per cent.
- Losses were running at roughly US$20 million a month after the firm stopped operations in June 2015 due to inability to pay its gas bill.

Pakistan Railways

- The net losses of Pakistan Railways went up by seven per cent to PKR32.52 billion in fiscal year 2014 from PKR30.5 billion in the previous financial year.
- The long term liabilities went up by 1.87 per cent to PKR74.12 billion in fiscal year 2013.

- Losses have been covered by grant-in-aid provided by the federal government.

INTERNATIONAL COMPARISONS

OECD Guidelines on Corporate Governance

The most comprehensive guidelines for the governance of SOEs were developed by OECD in 2004. These guidelines specifically address the following areas:

- ✓ **Ensuring an Effective Legal and Regulatory Framework for State-Owned Enterprises:** The legal and regulatory framework for state-owned enterprises should ensure a level playing field in markets where state-owned enterprises and private sector companies compete in order to avoid market distortions.
- ✓ **State Acting as an Owner**: State as a stakeholder in PSEs must be that of a vigilant owner.
- ✓ **Equitable Treatment of Shareholders**: Rights of shareholders shall be recognized and respected by the PSEs.
- ✓ **Relations with Stakeholders:** The state ownership policy should fully recognize the state-owned enterprises' responsibilities towards stakeholders and request that they report on their relations with stakeholders.
- ✓ **Transparency and Disclosure**: PSEs should ensure

that they are complying with the transparency and accountability guidelines provided by the OECD.

- ✓ **The Responsibilities of the Boards of State-Owned Enterprises (SOEs):** The Boards of state-owned enterprises should have the necessary authority, competence, and objectivity to carry out their function of strategic guidance and monitoring of management.

While these guidelines provide the underpinning of most SOE reforms around the world, it is instructive to study the differing implementation modalities employed in various jurisdictions.

Temasek – Singapore

The growing trend towards a centralized ownership model was spearheaded by Temasek of Singapore. Under this model, the shareholding of all SOEs is transferred to a government holding company or designated ministry. In Temasek's case, it is a national holding company for SOEs, registered under the Company Act. The Board of Temasek comprises nine members, five of whom are from the private sector. Under the Singapore constitution, neither the President nor the government of Singapore can be involved in its investment, divestment, or other business decisions. Temasek showed great resilience during the post-2007 period marked by economic downturn and since then this structure has gained great significance in international debate. The core values of Temasek's corporate governance model revolve around the following.

Figure 1: Key responsibilities of the Board of Directors under Temasek Guidelines for Corporate Governance

The above diagram reflects the key responsibilities that are to be shouldered by the BoD under Temasek Guidelines for Corporate Governance.

Key aspects of the Temasek guidelines include:

- ✓ PSE directors will be appointed for a one year probationary period.
- ✓ Key Performance Indicators to be introduced for the appraisal of organizations and directors, such as bottom lines and employee turnover.
- ✓ Private sector to be taken on board to help in policy making and implementation of the policies.

Khazanah Model – Malaysia

Like the Temasek Model of Corporate Governance, the Malaysian Khazanah Model is also considered one of the best examples of corporate governance for PSEs. There are a number of aspects that the Temasek and the Khazanah models have in common and this has ensured the sustainability of both models over the years. The Khazanah Model runs with the objective of providing value to shareholders on a consistent basis under the following principles of Corporate Governance. This model provides a valuable yardstick for defining the PSE Corporate Governance structure in Pakistan. Apart from the principles and pillars that are found in most Corporate Governance Models, Khazanah also incorporates some Key Performance Indicators that help monitor the performance of the BoDs and the PSEs in terms of quantifiable results.

Figure 2: The Khazanah Model

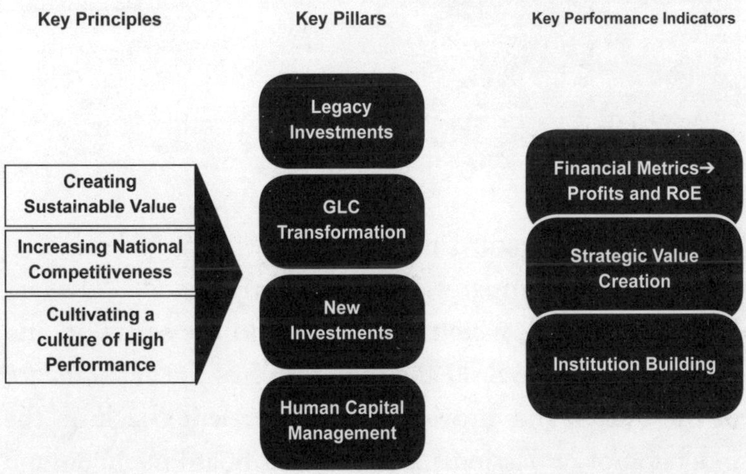

New Zealand – CCMAU, Crown Company Monitoring Advisory Unit

The CCMAU Model of Corporate Governance is based on the principles of accountability and transparency as shown in the figure below. Accountability is ensured through various levels of control.

Figure 3: State-owned enterprise governance in New Zealand

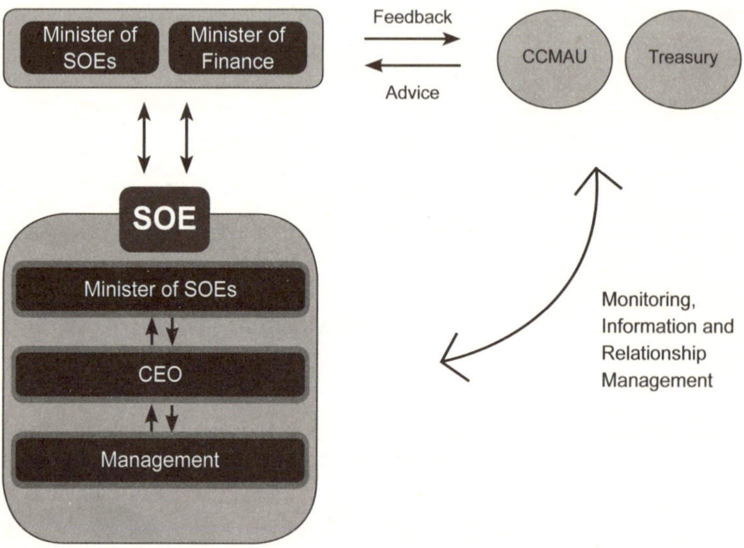

The unique feature in this model is the presence of the Crown Company for Monitoring and Advisory Unit (CCMAU), which is dedicated to the selection and nomination of the BoD and monitoring of the performance of the SOEs. This provides an independent check on the induction of professional and qualified Board members and minimizes the influence of line ministries in the day to day affairs of the SOEs.

Finland – Corporate Governance Structure and Practices

Finland initiated its reform of PSEs in the 1980s at a time when its PSEs accounted for nearly 20 per cent of the GDP, were poorly run, heavily indebted and financed by the state budget. Its reforms revolved around inducting professional non-executive boards in all companies and ensuring that they were run on a commercial basis. The following diagram shows the accountability structure for the ownership steering department responsible for the affairs of the PSEs.

Figure 4: Reformed PSE governance in Finland

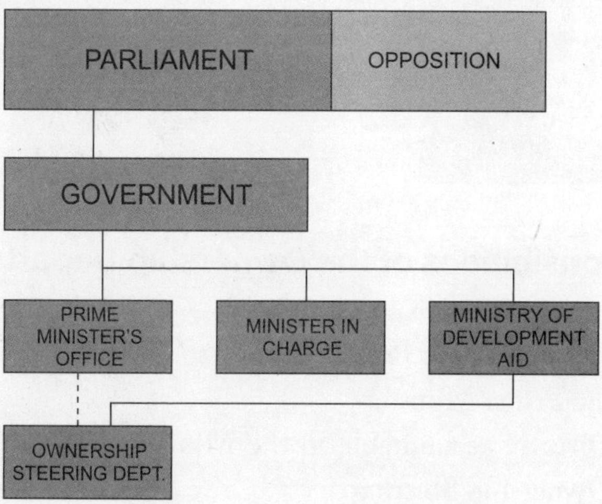

Key Principles of State Ownership Steering

- No separate state ownership code
- Principles of ownership in Government Resolution
- Separation of regulatory and ownership functions
- In listed companies, no state privileges
- Commercial companies run on commercial basis
    1. Efficiency and profitability
    2. State support measures equal to all
- In all companies professional non-executive board members
    1. No politicians, maximum one civil servant
- Candidate Bank

Figure 5: How ownership steering works

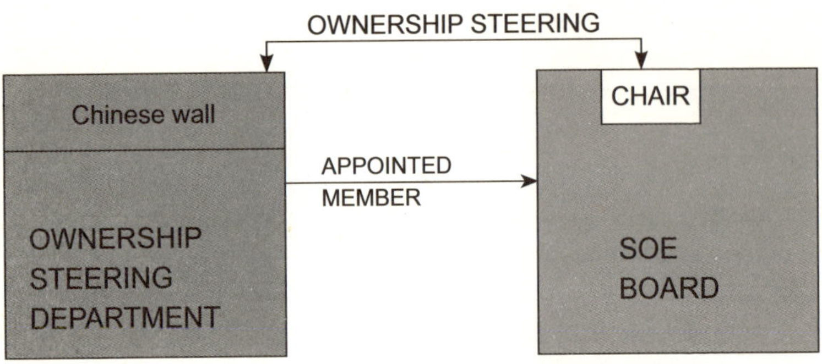

Responsibilities of the Ownership Department

- Located in the Prime Minister's Office, but not under the Prime Minister
- Directly accountable to the Minister responsible for Ownership Steering

Figure 6: A comparison of Temasek, Khazanah, CCMAU, and the Finnish models of corporate governance

	Temasek	Khazanah	New Zealand	Finland
Legal Structure	Incorporated in 1974 as an exempt private company	Incorporated in 1993 as an holding company, wholly owned by the ministry of finance	Each SOE has 2 Shareholding Ministers, each of whom own 50% of the company's shares. Shareholder's statutory powers in the company's act and SOE act	No separate ownership code. Principles of ownership in Government resolution State Adheres largely to the code for listed companies.
Board Composition	9 member (5 Private sector) Board assisted by 3 committees including LDCC*	8 member (5 from Private sector) Prime Minister chairman of the Board	Shareholding ministers appoint a BoD of each SOE with advice from CCMAU	Board consists of professional non-executive members and one civil servant as a regular member acting as only 'eyes and ears'. Dialogue with state conducted by chairman.
Accountability	President of Singapore	Prime Minister of Malaysia	Under SOE act shareholding ministers are responsible to the house of Representatives	Directly accountable to responsible minister through ownership steering department and indirectly to parliament.

*Leadership Development and Compensation Committee

- Ownership strategy, analyses and monitoring, legal matters and communications
- Independent organization enables sufficient ability to react and exercise criticism

The four models of Corporate Governance discussed so far have been summarized in the figure above. These models are compared in three major dimensions in the above diagram, namely Legal Structure; Board Composition; and Accountability. It is important to highlight these differences to show their practical applicability to the local environment in which they operate. All three aspects will be required to be dealt with in proposing a suitable structure in Pakistan's case.

CORPORATE GOVERNANCE GUIDELINES IN INDIA

Given the similarities in the cultural norms between India and Pakistan, it is important to study the Indian model as well. The following figure provides an analysis of how corporate governance in India is monitored and the yardsticks against which its performance is gauged.

These guidelines, though voluntary in nature, are followed by all Corporate Public Sector Enterprises (CPSEs) in India.

Proper implementation of these guidelines is intended to protect the interests of shareholders and relevant stakeholders.

Figure 7: Corporate governance for PSEs in India

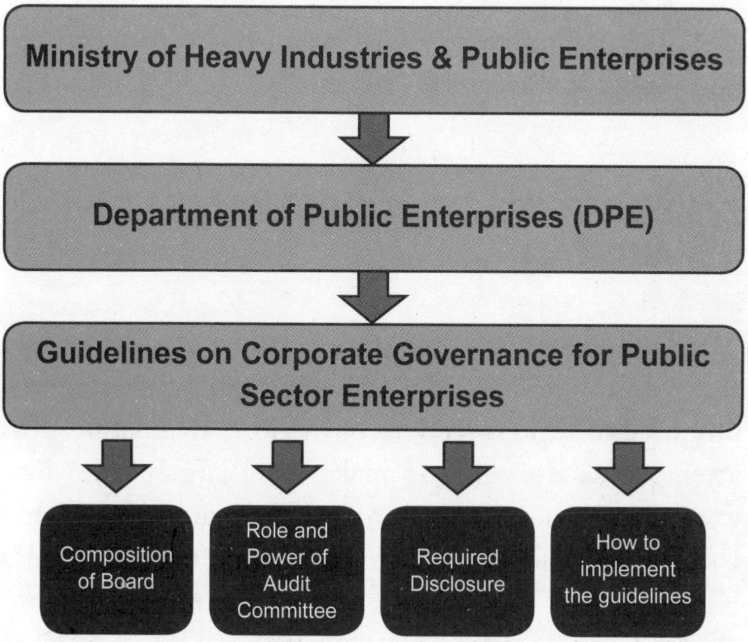

- The compliance with these guidelines are reflected in
    1. Directors' report,
    2. Annual Report
    3. Chairman's speech in the Annual General Meeting.
- DPE grades the CPSEs on the basis of their compliance with the corporate governance guidelines
- Quarterly evaluation is done by line ministries
- Annual reviews are carried out with the help of the DPE
- A special Task Force discusses PSE targets with both the CEO and line ministry concerned
- Yearly performances are first evaluated by the PSEs themselves, then sent to the DPE.

- Task Force evaluates compliance and performance on a scale of one to five.
- The performance of CEOs and Board members are linked to this score.

SALIENT FEATURES OF PSE GUIDELINES IN PAKISTAN

After an in-depth comparative study made between various jurisdictions, the following amendments were proposed to various sections of the PSE Regulations. An attempt was also made to make them largely consistent with the Corporate Governance Guidelines for Listed Companies in Pakistan, which have been revised recently. However, some differences remain, primarily because it was felt that PSEs need to face a higher level of accountability. In addition, the regulations take account of two additional features peculiar to PSEs: the reality of political interference in their day-to-day operations and the perceived dichotomy between their social and commercial objectives.

Definitions

- Comprehensive definition of 'Independent Director' consistent with Revised Code of Corporate Governance for listed companies.

Composition of the Board

- Majority of the Board as Independent Directors
- Appointing authority/government and other shareholders shall apply 'fit and proper criteria' in making nominations for election as Board members

Board Evaluation and Role

- Annual evaluation of the Board's performance
- Chairman will take leadership of the process
- Policy formulation and oversight and not the approval of individual transactions unless they are of an extraordinary nature or involve materially large amounts

Separation of Chairman and CEO

- Responsibilities of Chairman
  1. Leading the Board, ensuring its efficient and effective working, and setting its agenda
  2. Ensuring all directors are enabled and encouraged to fully participate in the deliberations and decisions of the Board.
  3. Should not be involved in day-to-day operations.
- Responsibilities of Chief Executive
  1. Management under the oversight of the Board.
  2. Implementation of strategies and policies approved by the Board.

3. Making appropriate arrangements to ensure that funds and resources are properly safeguarded and used economically, efficiently and effectively in accordance with any statutory obligations.

Directors to Act in the Best Interest of the Company (and not for their nominating organizations)

- Exercise their powers and carry out their fiduciary duties with a sense of objective judgment in the best interest of the company.
- This provision shall apply to all directors, including ex-officio directors.
- A director, once appointed/elected, shall hold office for a period of three years in accordance with the provisions of the Ordinance, unless he resigns or is removed in accordance with the provisions of the Ordinance.

Security of Tenure in Line with the Law

- Removal of a director should only take place in the event of misconduct or substandard performance determined through a performance evaluation.

Provisions Apply to Ex-officio Directors as well

- Obligations to all shareholders are fulfilled and they are duly informed in a timely manner of all material events through shareholder meetings and other communications
- Establish sound system of internal control

Board's Responsibilities with Regard to Code of Conduct

- 'Code of Conduct' for directors, executives and all employees, articulates acceptable and unacceptable behaviour
- Communication throughout the company including posting on the website
- Adequate controls for the identification and redressal of grievances arising from unethical practices
- Nominate a committee, a Board member or senior executive for investigating, where necessary, on a confidential basis, any deviation from the company's code of ethics

Conflict of Interest

- Directors and executives do not allow a conflict of interest to undermine their objectivity and they do not use their position to further their personal interest.
- Where actual or potential conflict of interest exists,

there should be appropriate identification, disclosure and management.

Anti-Corruption Policy

- A 'register of interests', which shall be publicly available.
- Board shall develop and implement a policy on 'anti-corruption' to minimize actual or perceived corruption in the company.

Related Party Transactions

- Comprehensive requirements on related party transaction disclosure and approval by the Audit Committee and the Board.

Power of Appointment of CEO must be Exercised by the Board

- Board shall exercise its power of: Appointment, development and succession of the CEO using 'fit and proper criteria', as well as other members of senior management.

Policies on Corporate Social Responsibility and Expenditure on GoP Directives

- Board Policies on:
  1. Corporate Social Responsibility initiatives including donations, charities, contributions and other payments of a similar nature;
  2. Where decisions are taken in fulfilling social objectives of the government but which are not in the commercial interest of the entity, appropriate subsidy must be extended by the government;
  3. Effective communication policy with all stakeholders.

Annual Report and Interim Financial Statements

- Quarterly accounts to be prepared and approved by the Board
- Annual report including annual financial statements must be placed on the website
- Monthly accounts, whether audited or otherwise, for circulation amongst the Board members

Orientation Courses

- Required to hold orientation courses; at least one orientation course per year
- Encouraged to have certification under an appropriate

director training/education programme offered by any institution, local or foreign

- From 30 June 2012 to 30 June 2016, every year minimum one director shall acquire the said certification.

Formation of Board Committees

- Formation of Board Committees, including Audit Committee, Risk Management Committee (for financial sector), HR Committee, and procurement committee
- Chaired by non-executive directors and the majority of their members should be independent
- Written terms of reference that defines their duties, authority and composition
- Carry out their performance evaluation on annual basis and submit such assessment to the Board
- Chairman of the Board shall take leadership role in ensuring completion of such evaluation process

CFO and Company Secretary

- Appointment, remuneration and terms and conditions of the Chief Financial Officer; the Company Secretary; and the Chief Internal Auditor shall be determined with the approval of the Board.
- Cannot be removed without Board approval
- CFO and Company Secretary to attend all Board

meetings, except where matters relating to them are discussed.

Company Secretary

- Responsible for ensuring that Board procedures are followed, and that all applicable statutes and regulations and other relevant statements of best practice are complied with.

Directors' Remuneration

- A formal and transparent procedure for fixing the remuneration packages of individual directors. No director shall be involved in deciding his own remuneration.
- Remuneration packages shall encourage value creation, and shall align their interest with the PSE.
- Require prior approval of shareholders
- Sufficient to attract and retain directors needed to run the company successfully
- Shall not be at a level perceived to compromise their independence
- Annual report shall contain criteria and details of remuneration of each director, including salary, benefits and performance-linked incentives.

RECOMMENDATIONS FOR PAKISTAN

While the ideal state for Corporate Governance of PSEs would be to move towards a centralized ownership structure, this may not be appropriate for Pakistan in terms of political will and ease of implementation. Therefore we are recommending the setting up of an independent committee to nominate, monitor, and determine remuneration of Board members. However, before discussing the implementation modalities for this, a certain amount of groundwork needs to be done to clarify Government's policy on PSEs and to ensure that the enabling environment is there for them to contribute effectively to the country's economy.

Develop a Clear PSE Policy

1. Decide on 'Whether it is the business of government to run business.' Reasons need to be enunciated for owning or controlling companies critical to Pakistan's security and economic well-being. Finland's experience in this regard is instructive. A rationalization of the current list of PSEs into those that are of strategic importance or those that are for special assignment is needed to focus the government's attention towards privatization or corporatization.
2. All remaining PSEs should be brought under standard legal structures. Corporatization would contribute to overall transparency by requiring proper compilation of accounts and information sharing.

3. Government as a shareholder needs to communicate what the objectives, role and mandate of PSEs ought to be and their expectation regarding operational and financial performance.

Create an Enabling Environment for Reform of PSEs

1. PSEs have to be managed on a sound commercial basis, separated from government's function of policy making, market regulation or social obligations. They also need to be held accountable to ensure judicious use of public resources. PSEs should make full disclosure of trade-offs they face in terms of costs and quality of delivery. The budget should annually provide for financing of the required shortfall or subsidies in a transparent manner.
2. State ownership should not entitle a competitive edge to PSEs so there is a need to create a level playing field and nurture contestability in markets. Competition forces firms to minimize costs and to search for new and better ways of doing business and this will enhance economic efficiency and innovation.
3. At the same time, there is a need to enhance the role and capacities of the sector regulators and the Competition Commission to examine the PSEs' role in transport, power generation and public utilities, which often operate as 'natural monopolies' (even if private entry is allowed) and examine whether state ownership is ensuring an adequate level of service provision.

Implementation Modality for PSE Reform

There is no institution better placed than the BoD to ensure good corporate governance at the entity level. Therefore the primary focus of Corporate Governance reform of PSEs needs to be on the selection of qualified and competent people on the BoDs of these entities. The appropriate mechanism needs to be put in place to ensure the right selection and continuous monitoring of the members of the Board, divorced from political interference. This mechanism could take the form of a separate government department, similar to the Department of Public Enterprises in India, or it could be outside the ambit of any particular ministry like the CCMAU in New Zealand. It could also evolve as a public-private sector partnership with the support of an international financial institution. Our recommendation is for the latter, so that the best skills in both the public and private sector can be tapped to take this important initiative forward.

The terms of reference for this Steering Committee for PSEs (SCPSE) will include:

1. Identification of candidates for the Boards of PSEs based on a 'fit and proper' criterion. This criterion has already been incorporated into the Guidelines for Corporate Governance of PSEs.
2. Initial screening of the candidates to ensure their fit within the relevant entity and their nomination to the relevant ministry. The line ministry will then select the proposed Board members from the list provided by the SCPSE. This may be more pragmatic, as it leaves

the discretion of appointments on the Boards to the relevant ministries, but only from people independently identified by the SCPSE, comprising appropriately qualified and experienced individuals.

3. Determine the remuneration based on market analysis. The remuneration levels as communicated in the guidelines ensure that they compensate the members of the Board adequately for their time and expertise, yet are not at a level that can be perceived to compromise their independence.
4. Monitor the performance of the Board. This evaluation is periodically carried out by the Board and shared with the SCPSE so that the members remain accountable to a monitoring body after their selection to a Board. The Boards should also be fully empowered to appoint the CEO and senior management, carry out their performance appraisal and report to the Ministry and the Nominating Board on an annual basis that they have done so. Based on the reports received, the SCPSE should provide their feedback/input to the relevant ministries.
5. The recommendation to terminate the services of a member of the Board should also be endorsed by the SCPSE based on performance evaluation.
6. Collate the operational and financial performance and service standards offered vis-a-vis the corporate strategy and benchmarks.
7. Develop a score card that both the listed and other PSE undertakings adopt and report their compliance relative to the Corporate Governance Code.

8. Offer online this information to the public as well as the performance of comparative companies.

COMPOSITION OF THE SCPSE

As mentioned, the SCPSE needs to be comprised of members from both the public and private sector to ensure the appropriate mix of skills as well as to ensure ownership of the process across a broader spectrum. Senior people from the business community with experience of corporate Boards, bureaucrats and professionals need to be tapped for the SCPSE, applying the same fit and proper criteria developed for individual Boards of PSEs. Ex-officio membership from ministries should be discouraged, as should institutional representation. It is also recommended that members of the regulatory bodies should not be part of the SCPSE since it may compromise their role as regulators of the entity for which they were responsible for selecting the Board members.

FUNDING OF THE SCPSE

It is recommended that this SCPSE be funded through an initial grant provided by an international financial institution and sustained through annual disbursement made by the Ministry of Finance. The initial set-up costs would comprise the allocation for a small secretariat including personnel and IT resources. The secretariat would coordinate between the SCPSE and the relevant ministries, solicit and compile the database of candidates, and solicit and maintain a database for the financial performance of PSEs. Overall it will be responsible for supporting compliance with the terms of reference of the SCPSE under the guidance of the Chair of the SCPSE. The working capital over time will include the remuneration of the members of the SCPSE as well who will be inducted for specified terms.

The accountability structure proposed for the SCPSE is illustrated in the diagram below:

Figure 8: Proposed accountability structure for the SCPSE

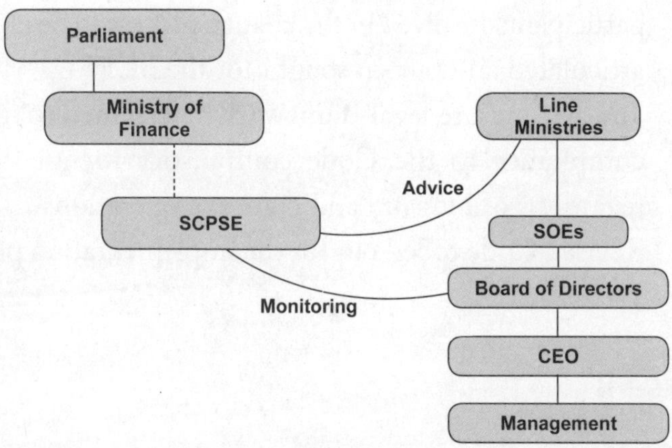

TIMELINE

It is recommended that a phased approach be undertaken for implementation to ensure appropriate sequencing of events and to generate adequate ownership of the process.

Phase I

Phase I will focus on the conceptualization of the appropriate framework and its articulation:

1. Finalizing of the Code of Corporate Governance for PSEs through appropriate public feedback that has been concluded with the notification of the Public Sector Companies Corporate Government Rules 2013
2. Categorization of different types of PSEs with the aim of bringing them under a common legal structure
3. Roles and responsibilities of government and the participants involved in the change process to be clearly articulated and buy-in sought for the SCPSE
4. The appropriate legal framework determined to make compliance to the Code compulsory for all PSEs regardless of industry and nature of operations
5. Revised Code rolled out for the implementation phase

Phase II

Phase II includes the implementation phase:

1. Set up the Steering Committee for PSEs (SCPSE)
2. Appoint members of the SCPSE charged with the task of nominating and monitoring the boards of PSEs
3. Institutionalize framework for periodic monitoring of all PSEs

4. Exercise constant quality checks to ensure compliance of the PSEs with the Code of Corporate Governance
5. Undertake impact analysis of new policies on the economic performance of the PSEs and on Pakistan's economy
6. Propose corrective measures where required

The above two phases can be graphically summarized as follows:

Table 1: Timeline for PSE governance reform in Pakistan

Time	PHASE I	Time	PHASE II
Period 1	Political Will/Public Debate	Period 6	Steering Committee
Period 2	Categorization	Period 7	Appointments
Period 3	Roles and Responsibilities	Period 8	Periodic Evaluation
Period 4	Legal Framework	Period 9	Impact Analysis
Period 5	Code	Period 10	Corrective Measures

These recommendations have been made keeping in mind that some of the more successful centralized models of governance discussed earlier may be premature and impractical in Pakistan's milieu. However, if the above corrective measures prove inadequate to stem the rapid deterioration in the PSEs, a more radical shift towards centralized ownership models may be required. As with all reform measures, the implementation has to be in 'letter and spirit' so that its chances of success are not sacrificed at the altar of political expediency.

Postscript

The Public Sector Companies Corporate Governance Rules were notified by the Securities & Exchange Commission of Pakistan in 2013 with the approval of the federal government. While no Steering Committee to oversee its implementation has been created, the SECP itself has attempted to ensure compliance through a 'statement of compliance' that is expected to be submitted by each PSE along with its annual report. As of June 2015, 37 per cent of PSEs had submitted their statement of compliance, up from 14 per cent the previous year. While progress has been gradual, the absence of a coordinated effort to apply the fit and proper criteria in the induction of qualified, competent professionals on the Boards of these PSEs has perpetuated the chasm between the 'letter and intent' of these Rules.

Notes

1. The paper was initially prepared in 2012 as part of a consultancy for the Centre for International Private Enterprise (CIPE), Pakistan, to assist the Steering Committee convened by the Ministry of Finance to draft the Rules for Public Sector Enterprises.
2. Data collated from various newspaper reports between 2014–16.

PART II

Enshrined Principles: Towards Greater Responsibility, Accountability, and Transparency

Chapter 4

Building an Effective and Efficient Board

Sadia Khan

'There is no institution better placed to ensure good governance of corporations than the Board of Directors. But a Board consists of people, and a good Board consists of good people, with the integrity to do what's right, with the competence to contribute, with the stature to stand up to management when necessary, and with a sense of responsibility to all shareholders regardless of their size. It is this people factor that has seen most codes left as guidelines rather than being formulated as rules.'[1]

In this chapter, we discuss what it takes to build an effective and efficient Board, with the right structure, composition, and understanding of Board procedures.

1. BOARD COMPOSITION AND STRUCTURE:

Given the impact of Board structure and composition on its performance, it is important to discuss the factors determining the number of directors on a Board, the right mix of skills as well as the right mix of categories, i.e. executive, non-executive, or independent.

However, it is important first to gain some understanding of the primary role of Board members.

Figure 1: The 'Emotional Climate' of the Board

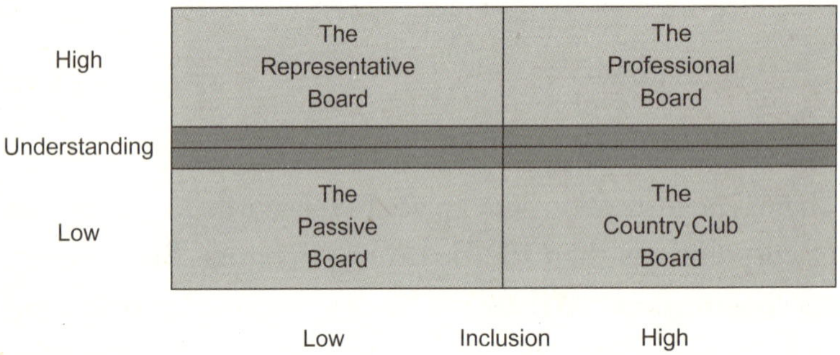

Source: Bob Garret (2003) Thin on Top—Why Corporate Governance Matters and How to Measure and Improve Board Performance

Powers, Duties, and Obligations of Directors under Code of Corporate Governance

- Vision, mission and strategy
- Stewardship (responsibility towards stakeholders and accountability)
- Board operations
- Maintenance of proper records to enable extraction of financial statements.
- Establishment of adequate internal controls
- Application of accounting policies

- Safeguarding the assets of the company
- Fair presentation of financial statements
- Developing corporate culture
- Monitoring and evaluation
- Financial reporting
- Compliance
- Prepare 'Statement of Ethics and Business Practices' annually to establish a standard of conduct for directors and employees. The Statement has to be signed by each director and employee.
- Formulation of significant policies and maintenance of record thereof.
- Borrowing of moneys and the amount in excess of which borrowings shall be sanctioned/ratified by a general meeting of shareholders.

Since the Board needs to be an effective decision-making body, its size is an important factor. Companies choose a Board size that enables them to bring skill sets required to direct the company, bring diversity in experience, and efficiently organize the Board committee work. The determining factors for the size of the Board include the nature and complexity of the business, and the number of sub-committees needed to undertake the work of the Board efficiently and diligently.

Ideally, large listed companies typically have between eight to twelve directors on their Board. It is significant that the trend in countries such as the US, and now even in Japan, appears to be towards smaller Boards. Average Board size in the largest companies ranges from 11 members in Latin America to over 23 members in Japan, as shown in the table on the next page.

Figure 2: Average sizes of one-tier or supervisory boards by region

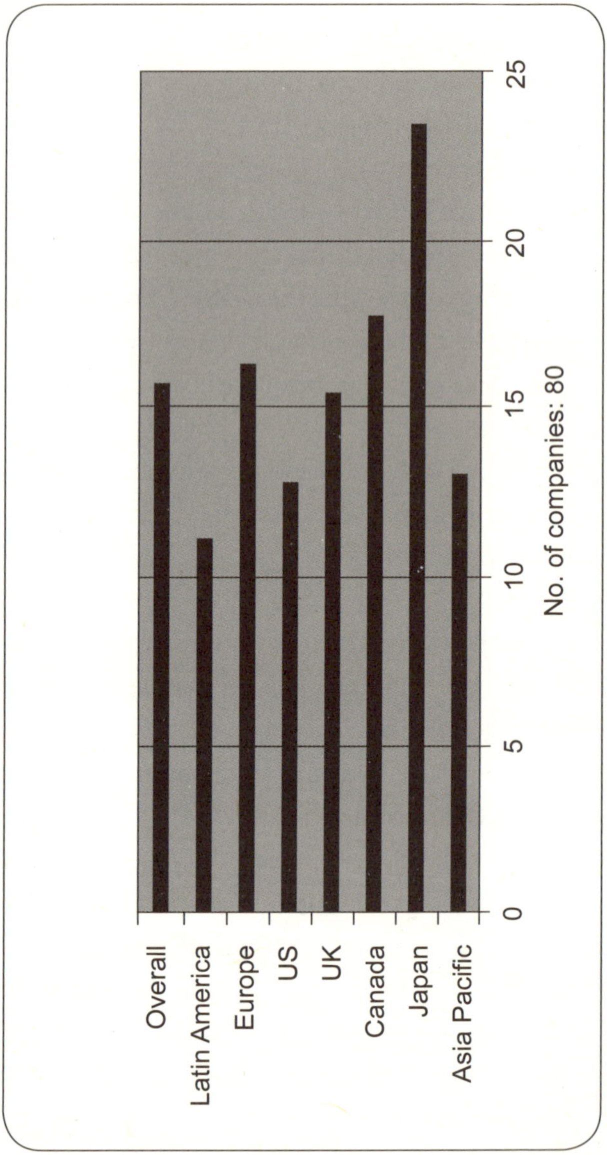

It should be noted that a change in the number of directors may change the existing balance of power, which is why an Annual General Meeting that takes that decision is very often quite turbulent and distracts shareholders from other important issues. For this reason, it would be advisable to have the charter regulate the size of the Board. In Pakistan, the size of a Board is regulated by Section 174 of the Companies Ordinance, whereby private companies should have two or more directors and public companies should have seven or more directors.

According to the Higgs Report, an effective Board should not be so large as to become unwieldy. It should be of sufficient size that the balance of skills and experience is appropriate for the requirements of thc business and that changes in the Board's composition can be managed without undue disruption.

Finding the right mix of skills and competence is an equally challenging task. The following chart depicts some of the personal characteristics as well as industry experience that is considered critical in getting the right mix of people with integrity and business acumen in arriving at informed decision making at a collective level. Many of these characteristics have made their way into formalized 'fit and proper' criteria devised by the State Bank of Pakistan for use in appointing Board directors within the financial sector.

Figure 3: Board member skills and competencies

Finding the Right Mix of Skills and Competencies for the Board

Competencies

- Industry Experiences
- Business Judgment
- Education/Special Skills, for example:
  - Finance and Accounting;
  - Risk Management and Internal Control; or
  - Strategic Management.

Personal Characteristics

- Leadership
- Integrity
- Accountability
- Maturity
- Work Ethic
- Time
- Courage

Qualification of a Board Member

Subject to eligibility criteria in the Companies Ordinance 1984 and any of the relevant legislation, the following could be indicative profile specifications for Board members:

- Experience: Serving on other Boards.
- Achievements: Successful in business, public service, or profession.
- Skills: Talents and skills contribution to the Board.

Complement the skills of the Board members, fill any existing gap in Board member skills.

- Personal qualities: Good listener with ability to prioritize issues; good inter-personal skills, balanced perspective.
- Integrity: The individual must exemplify high ethical and moral standards in personal and business life.
- Commitment: The individual must remain committed to the organization and Board over the tenure.
- Objectivity: The individual must be sufficiently independent so that he or she can consider issues from an open and unbiased perspective.
- Willingness to be trained: The individual must be open to learning and being trained about the organization and about Board responsibilities.
- Available time: The individual must be able to devote adequate time to serving on the Board.

Continuous Learning

- Enhancement of individual and collective capabilities and skills

Continuous Improvement

- Selective use of advice and guidance; focus on informed, professional sources

Adding Value

- Making positive contributions for benefit of stakeholders

Independent Feedback

- Key to improved performance

Exchange Ideas

- Networking in-house and external peers and colleagues

SBP's Fit and Proper Test

- **Integrity, Honesty and Reputation**
  - Not convicted of fraud, forgery, or financial crime
  - No adverse findings in civil/criminal proceedings, particularly investment, financial misconduct, fraud, etc.
  - Not involved in companies whose licence has been revoked or gone into liquidation because of mismanagement/malpractice

- **Track Record**
  - Impeccable track record
  - Not demoted/dismissed/forced to resign from bank/DFI
- Solvency and Financial Integrity
  - Not involved in illegal financial dealings
  - Not a defaulter in payment of dues or taxes
- Qualifications and Experience
  - Active Management/Business experience of at least five years
  - Graduation, preferably in banking/finance

- **Conflict of Interest**
  - Not a director of any other bank/DFI (NIT nominees excluded)

- Holding substantial interest or working in key position of exchange company, Member of Stock Exchange and Corporate Brokerage House, etc.
- Not consultant or advisor to company

2. TYPES OF DIRECTORS AND THEIR LEADERSHIP ATTRIBUTES

There are primarily three types of director: Executive, Non-Executive, and Independent.

Executive Directors

Executive Directors hold an operational position/are on the payroll of the company.

These directors simultaneously serve as members of the company executive management. Their role is to help approve strategy, improve information flows, foster teamwork (rather than an 'us-vs-them' attitude), and facilitate accountability (e.g. receive direction). In Pakistan, where the CEO is deemed to be a Board member, it helps to raise the profile of the CEO as well. There is a greater risk of distortion or withholding of information or lack of balance in the management contribution to the Boardroom debate when there are few or no executive directors.

Non-Executive Directors

Non-Executive directors do not hold an executive position and they may or may not be independent. These Board members are not members of the company's executive management. Their role is to constructively challenge management, contribute to strategy development, monitor performance of management, monitor financial controls and risk management, remuneration, nomination and succession planning, share in decision-making, hire and fire the CEO. Non-executive directors bring a dispassionate objectivity that directors with a closer relationship to the company cannot provide.

Independent Directors

These are non-executive, outside directors who meet the criteria for independence. Independent directors are responsible for determining appropriate levels of remuneration for executive directors, have a prime role in appointing, and where necessary removing, senior management, and in succession planning. Independent directors constructively challenge and contribute to the development of strategy, scrutinize the performance of management in meeting agreed upon goals and objectives, and monitor the reporting of performance. They should satisfy themselves that financial information is accurate, and that financial controls and systems of risk management are robust and defensible.

Legal Requirements in Pakistan on Board Composition

Executive Directors:

- SBP regulation for financial institutions/banks: maximum two members of the Board, including Chief Executive, can be Executive directors.
- CG Code: Executive directors not more than 75 per cent of the elected directors in listed companies.

Non-executive Directors

- SBP regulation: in case of family members, not more than 25 per cent.
- CG Code: Non-executive directors, not less than 25 per cent of directors in listed companies.

Independent Directors

- SBP regulation: not less than 25 per cent of directors to be independent.
- CG Code: At least one independent director.

Why Independent Directors are Important

According to the OECD Global Corporate Governance Principles of 2004, while responsibility for financial reporting, remuneration and nomination are those of the Board as a whole, independent non-executive Board members can provide additional assurance to market participants so that their interests are defended; so much so that the Higgs Report defines certain criteria for ensuring independence. These include:

'Independent in character and judgement, no relationships or circumstances which could affect, or appear to affect, the director's judgement.

- Former employee of the company until five years after employment or material connection had ended
- Has had material business relationship with company within the past three years
- Receives additional remuneration from company apart from director's fee, i.e. share options, pension scheme
- Has close family ties with advisers, directors, senior employees of company
- Holds cross–directorships or significant links with other directors through involvement in other companies
- Represents significant shareholder
- Has served on the Board for more than ten years.'

Legal requirements in Pakistan for independence dictate that:

1. A director who is not connected with the listed company or its promoters or directors on the basis of family relationship; and
2. Who does not have any other relationship [...] with the listed company, its associated companies, directors, executives or related parties.

Stress test of independence: Can such a person be reasonably perceived as being able to exercise independent business judgment without being subservient to any form of interference?

Any person nominated as a director under sections 182 and 183 of the Companies Ordinance of 1984 shall not be taken to be an 'independent director'.

The State Bank of Pakistan goes one step further and brings the criteria of independence for Board members of financial sector companies more in line with the criteria specified in the Higgs Report.

- Not linked directly or indirectly with bank/DFI or its sponsor/strategic shareholders.
- Not been employed by the bank/DFI within the last five years.
- Not been an employee or affiliate of present/former auditor, consultant, legal advisor within the last three years.
- Not been an employee of subsidiary or associate company where directors have substantial beneficial interest (20 per cent or more).

- Not employed in company where executive officer of bank/DFI has been a director within the last three years.
- Not affiliated with not-for-profit entity that receives contributions over 10 million or 2 per cent of its gross revenues.
- Independent director submits declaration of independence to SBP at time of appointment.

3. DIRECTOR SELECTION AND REMUNERATION

Given the importance of getting the right mix of skills and competence on the Board, it is obvious that the selection process itself should be rigorous and comprehensive. Unfortunately, few companies invest time and effort in institutionalizing a selection process suitable to their requirements. In the absence of Boards' involvement in succession planning, the chances are that when the time comes, Boards simply endorse the nominee of the controlling shareholder. Planning and developing future leadership is crucial for the long term and sustained success of a company. For a fair and reliable system it is important for the Board or a Board Committee to oversee this activity and provide an annual review for the benefit of the entire Board.

The first step in the process is the establishment of a non-executive, ideally independent, nominations committee, which sets policy and recommends nominees. It should be remembered that Board committees are formed to assist the work of the entire Board, not to substitute it. They generally enjoy no executive powers, are focused on specialized areas of responsibility, with chair and members normally 'independent'. The key committees include Audit (sometimes includes risk), HR or Remuneration, and Nominations or Governance.

When forming a sub-committee focusing on specialized areas of Board responsibilities, the Board should define its terms of reference and limitations. In the discharge of various technical areas of Board responsibility, the sub-committees can call upon additional expertise, allow detailed interrogation of cases presented to them for consideration, and engage management in its deliberations.

The Nominations committee is typically charged with the identification of a Board capability gap: the Board or the Nominations committee should identify the knowledge, skills and personal attributes that a director would need to possess in order to fill this gap.

Development of a search plan: The Nominations committee should develop a search plan and lead the search process. This may involve the use of search consultants and the position may be advertised.

Familiarity with the candidates: The Nominations committee members will need to interview candidates. The terms and conditions of the position will be discussed, along with their time commitment.

Selection of the best qualified candidate: Finally the candidate should be presented for election at the general assembly and adequate information shared with the shareholders to facilitate informed decision making.

In determining non-executive remuneration, it is best to conduct a market survey of comparative companies. Two common methods for determining non-executive director compensation are:

- Pro-rata time valued at par with Executive Directors.
- Pro-rata time valued at par with key company consultants.

It is important to bear in mind that no one should be setting his/her own compensation. Excessive compensation impinges on independence of directors and it is important to make full disclosure to shareholders of compensation offered to the Board members.

4. BOARD: BEST PRACTICES

Conducting an Effective Board Meeting

Following points to be considered to conduct an effective Board meeting:

- Provide adequate advance notice of the meeting.
- Prepare a realistic agenda and supporting documents and deliver them to Board members at least one week before the meetings.
- Start and conclude the meeting promptly.
- Introduce any guests, observers, or new members. Be familiar with items on the agenda.
- Address action items first and items that require more discussion second.

- Stick to the agenda and not get side-tracked on other issues.
- Use parliamentary rules of order, but be flexible to achieve a consensus.
- Delegate to the Board committees responsibility for overseeing detailed, time-consuming work requiring investigation and analysis.
- Summarize the discussion on each point, identify the course of action and assign responsibility for action.
- Write up the minutes of the meeting immediately afterwards and distribute them while the meeting is fresh in people's memories.

Maintaining Focus, and Board Evaluation

- Institutionalize by having systems in place for:
    - o Implementation plan and checklist
    - o Independent feedback mechanism (monitoring compliance, e.g. ICAP's checklist)
    - o Board's assessment (overall performance)
    - o Individual directors' assessment
    - o Development programmes (training)
    - o New inductees' orientation programmes.
    - o Tool kit for Board members:
    - o Good practice approaches to corporate governance
    - o Job descriptions
    - o Checklists and questionnaires to help directors fulfil their duties

- Assign responsibility for the above tasks
- A Board committee could be set up for this purpose
- Board Information System (BIS) for monitoring compliance with Code of Corporate Governance.

The above checklists have been developed to provide some guidance on effective Board procedures. In practice, a lot depends on where the Board positions itself along the axis of its inclusiveness and in its understanding of corporate affairs. The right kind of skill mix and competence level will undoubtedly help the Board to bridge the gap between passivity and professionalism.

Note

1. The material for this chapter has been drawn primarily from the Board Development Series Programme prepared by consultants engaged by the IFC and lectures conducted by the PICG.

Chapter 5

Providing Strategic Leadership

The Board's Role in the Governance of a Company's Strategy

Tabish Gauhar

The shareholders invest in the capital of, and own, the company; they exercise their ownership rights by voting on resolutions in general meetings of the company and appoint the directors. However, for all practical purposes, the Board of Directors (Board) manages the company's affairs for and on behalf of the shareholders, for which the shareholders delegate powers to the Board under the statute and company's articles of association within the statutory limits and subject to certain shareholders' approvals. The Board, by and large, enjoys almost all the powers to make and implement strategic and policy decisions upholding the interests of the company. The responsibilities always follow and are commensurate with the authority mandate. The Board is fundamentally responsible for safeguarding and enhancing shareholder value and stewardship of the company's assets.

The Board plays a pivotal role in the governance of the company's strategy. In fact, the performance of the company, value addition in the long term and image building largely depend on the quality and key features of the corporate governance policy that the Board is pursuing. A properly focused Board has a clear understanding of and sets its role in between the role, responsibilities, activities and powers of the management and the shareholders. The Board recognizes, in letter and spirit, that its role is to direct and guide and not to manage and therefore does not involve itself in day-to-day management of the company and it simultaneously recognizes that they, as the Board of Directors, are accountable to the shareholders and therefore avoid taking decisions that are reserved for the shareholders in order to avoid legal infringement and ensure transparency.

The Board limits its role and sets its principal focus on strategic direction, key policy framework, long-term business plan, oversight and control, enhancing shareholder value, and corporate governance. The Board reviews and approves financial performance and financial statements with the main focus on the auditors' report/observations, business policies and practices, ethics, values and code of conduct, annual budget and major capital expenditure programmes, internal controls, governance and compliance framework. The directors exercise managerial oversight and provide strategic guidance, whereas the management and the performance of the company is the responsibility of the executives. Through this balanced and prudent approach, the Board not only avoids overlap controversies and auditors/regulators' questions but also places itself in a much better position to build and improve shareholders' value, key performance indicators, and the company's image. An overview of corporate sector performance across the world reveals that the successes and failures of companies fundamentally depend on their Board's insight, vision and the ability to visualize and plan beyond the near future. In short, the Board's proactive, selective and effective role in the governance of the company's strategy will decide the future of the company and its position among contemporaries at the national and regional level.

EFFECTIVE STRATEGY FORMULATION

The first and foremost action point is to develop a vision of the company that should essentially be aligned to the defined objectives of the company and disseminated across the company in order to have a clear understanding at all levels and inculcate commitment and sincerity of purpose. It is imperative that the charter of the company invariably supports and supplements key features and objectives outlined in its vision and mission statement. At times, the Board's aspirations and future outlook of the company are not reflected and incorporated in the company's charter and when the Board decides to implement an element of its strategic initiatives, it suddenly finds that the said objective is not adequately defined in the charter. This leads to the lengthy and cumbersome exercise of amending the charter, which eventually evaporates the essence and benefits of striking at the right time.

COMPOSITION OF THE BOARD

The selection and composition of the Board is the foundation on and around which the corporate governance structure of a company is built. Each and every director must have complete faith in the objectives, vision and mission of the company. Any conflict of interest must be properly addressed and an understanding and good working relationship among the directors without compromising on principle, honest judgment and the company's interests would ensure the smooth functioning of the company. The Board as a body must possess core competencies to formulate the company's strategy, guide, supervise and implement, monitor and analyse management performance, risk assessment, and mitigation and other governance actions. Individual directors with professional qualification, specialized knowledge, expertise and experience commensurate with the business wings and key activity areas of the company would lead them to be a part of various Board committees to positively contribute in achieving the company's objectives. The directors must be aware of their role and responsibilities, powers and duties and the provisions of the governing statutes and regulations thereof. The directors must perform their duties with a fiduciary and trusteeship mindset. Self-regulation, self-accountability and setting the examples of disciplined attitude, observance of code of conduct in letter and spirit will disseminate positive signals down the line.

The Board's foresight with a futurist outlook plays a decisive role in formulating the company's governance strategy. The Board should keep itself abreast of national, regional and international developments on technology, finance, IT, corporate governance and other areas impacting the business of the company and the challenges and opportunities likely to be forthcoming. The Board as a body should, as an integral component of its strategy and policy, keep on improving and updating directors' knowledge and skills through orientation courses and training programmes. The Board's long-term vision in wider perspective is one of the key components in formulating the company's strategy, as management is normally influenced by short-term business gains and is restricted to the local environment.

The other key areas that are normally ignored by the management include image building, Corporate Social Responsibility (CSR) policy and initiatives and Health, Education, Safety, and Environmental issues. The Board should ensure that the company effectively plays its role as a responsible corporate citizen and positively contributes to communities in health, education, social and environmental uplift and especially in the hours of crisis arising due to natural and other calamities.

The Board, as a part of the company's strategy, should further ensure selection and appointment at key management positions in a fair, competitive and transparent manner. The management team must possess core competencies in their respective fields and simultaneously enjoy a good reputation, integrity and ethical and moral values and complete faith in the objectives and policies of the company.

EVALUATING STRATEGY DELIVERY

The Board should ensure that all key policies of the company and power delegation framework are extensively reviewed at various levels and finally discussed and approved in a Board meeting. Any amendment in the said policies must also be approved by the Board. The Board should ensure that a comprehensive and effective control and monitoring mechanism and analytical, reporting and accountability processes are in place. Board committees, statutory and business-specific, should be constituted, comprising directors with related exposure, competence and skills. Terms of Reference (ToR) of various Board committees need to be properly defined, striking a judicious balance between powers and responsibilities and envisaging a clear reporting framework.

A sound system of internal controls and its effective and consistent implementation and vigilant monitoring, review and process updating make easy the Board's function to supervise strategy delivery and organizational performance. The Board should set up an independent internal audit (IA) function in the company headed by a professional internal auditor who should functionally report to the Board Audit Committee. The internal audit function should be suitably placed in the company and its human, technological and other resources should be adequately allocated. The scope of the internal audit function should be clearly defined and communicated across the company, aiming to develop mutual understanding, trust, a conducive environment and team spirit to achieve common objectives.

IA's role broadly entails review and evaluation of internal control systems in accordance with business risk assessment, which invariably includes assessment and evaluation of effectiveness and efficiency of operations, reliability of financial reporting, deterring and investigating fraudulent practices, safeguarding assets of the company and continual compliance with applicable statutes, regulations, standards and codes. The charter of internal audit may include undertaking special studies, consulting and investigating assignments and special projects as and when advised by the Board Audit Committee (BAC). Joint venture audit in collaboration with a Joint Venture partner with or without engaging independent consultants constitutes an important audit activity aiming to safeguard thc company's interest in joint ventures. A strong control environment with established internal control framework supported by IT-based systems and processes and built-in trigger mechanisms provides adequate assurance and is a useful tool for the Board to oversee organizational performance and intervene at the right place and time to safeguard the company's interests. The internal control framework is essentially based on a clear structure, segregation of duties, administrative and financial authority limits and other controls aimed at reducing the risk of undetected error, fraudulent activities and mismanagement, misstatement and misappropriation.

Selection and appointment of statutory (external) auditors on the BAC's recommendation and with shareholders' approval is equally important to strengthen the corporate governance structure of the company. The Board's meaningful participation in the process will augment the control structure.

The role of the BAC is of critical importance in developing and strengthening the overall control environment and risk identification, assessment and mitigation process. The BAC guides, supervises and coordinates with internal and external auditors and formulates objective recommendations for consideration of the Board. Internal audit reports are regularly presented to the BAC and audit findings and observations are discussed at length alongside management response, and remedial operational actions and amendment in policies are suggested. The BAC, at times, arranges Quality Assurance Review (QAR) of the internal audit function in order to assess and improve the IA function by engaging external consultants, in terms of international standards in a regional perspective. The BAC also interacts with and engages external auditors in extensive discussions on their report to the shareholders, Board of Directors, and in compliance with corporate governance standards. The Board as an integral component of evaluating delivery strategy should place its main focus on the BAC's reports, observations, findings and recommendations of the internal and external auditors to identify key issues besetting the company, adequacy or otherwise of internal controls and risk mitigation policy, and suggest remedial measures and policy amendments. Internal and external auditors may occasionally be invited to Board meetings in order to have direct discussions on key issues.

The Board, after ensuring that key policies, code of conduct, corporate structure, core committees, key management positions and internal controls are in place, switches over to its fundamental role to monitor and analyse organizational performance and effectiveness of management's actions and governing policy framework, re-assessment, and corrective measures where necessary.

The Board must ensure that the following key documents are submitted to it in a timely manner:

1. Annual and long-term business plan
2. Annual revenue and capital budget
3. Quarterly and annual financial statements, auditors' reports and any observations
4. All material transactions, significant issues and policy decisions
5. Update on any amendments in governing legal framework, statute, regulations and codes
6. Details and update on key litigation and regulatory and labour issues.

Simultaneously, the Board should ensure that only significant issues in the form of an Executive Summary supported only by relevant documents, objective analysis, and specific recommendations of the management/Board committees are coming to it. At times, unnecessary and irrelevant documents are sent to the Board in sizeable volume, which is counterproductive for the Board's decision making process. Working papers on agenda items for consideration in Board meetings should be circulated well in advance to the directors for their review, input, and meaningful discussions in the Board meeting. The Board meetings calendar should be finalized and circulated at the beginning of each financial year, facilitating the directors to schedule their travel plans or attending through teleconferencing. Efforts should be made that all or a maximum number of directors attend the Board meetings for the purpose of collective decision making on key policy issues. Detailed presentations should be made on agenda items to the Board by respective group/committee heads, queries of the directors be properly responded to and observations/suggestions properly noted, discussed and decided. Once the minutes of the meeting are finalized and circulated to the directors, the Board's decisions and directives should be communicated to the respective group head for compliance within the timeframe advised by the Board. Alongside should be an implementation report to be prepared by the Company Secretary that covers all decisions and actionable points taken in the Board meeting and identifying the delivery responsibility and timeline. The said report is circulated amongst the group heads involved in the execution process, advising to initiate the implementation measures and complete the action within the mentioned timeframe and submit a compliance report. In case the action is not concluded, a progress report will be submitted. Additionally, the following should also be submitted to the Board on a regular basis, normally at the end of each quarter:

1. Key Performance Indicators (KPIs) during review period and comparison with budget and actual in corresponding period last year. The above details are normally part of the presentation in quarterly financial statements.
2. A detailed working and comprehensive variance analysis of key operational and financial numbers in

the above three sets of figures, elaborating the reasons and justification for deviation.

3. A detailed analysis of achievements of budget targets with main focus on KPIs and under/over utilization of funds allocated for Capital Expenditure (CAPEX) projects. Under-utilization of funds allocated for major CAPEX projects is also a point of concern for the Board as it negatively impacts the long term business plan and revenue growth in a sustained manner in long term perspective and also results in cost escalations. This phenomenon, therefore, also needs to be carefully reviewed and properly fixed by the Board.
4. Reports and recommendations of all Board statutory and project-specific committees.
5. Brief update and way forward on all other significant and policy issues, which obviously vary from company to company and from time to time.

The above database, working papers, reports and recommendations constitute the key tool in evaluating delivery strategy in relation to policies and action plans approved and targets and timelines set by the Board.

The Board needs to set its main focus on the following evaluation techniques:

1. Milestone dates and milestone payments are in accordance with project timelines approved by the Board. Delays and cost overruns and reasons and justification thereof should be carefully analysed, responsibility fixed, and any negligence must lead to

an investigation and accountability process. Alongside, remedial steps be initiated forthwith to arrest and correct the deficiency.

2. There are always company-specific elements and key indicators such as product range, customer base, geographical placement, supply and demand curve, system losses and pilferage, seasonal impact and others, which materially impact the bottom line of the company's Profit and Loss Account. The Board should devise a standard template to objectively analyse such key ingredients in operational and financial performance of the company, duly backed by an accountability process and rectification measures.

The Chairman evaluates the performance of individual directors on the basis of his/her attendance in Board/ committee meetings, level of participation and input, and formulating suggestions and recommendations to add value and improve organizational performance, observance of code of conduct, disclosure of interest, integrity and moral and ethical standards. The Chairman meets and consults the directors, especially non-executive and independent ones, on a regular basis to discuss corporate governance issues, performance of the company and conducive environment enabling the directors to fulfil their fiduciary duties. The Board, as a body under the leadership of the Chairman, makes sure with the Chief Executive and Company Secretary that the Board is kept properly informed, is consulted on all issues reserved for it, and that its decisions are made in a timely and considered way that conforms to the corporate governance framework.

The Board needs to evaluate its own performance in an objective manner on a regular basis, which should essentially be based on overall organizational performance, implementation of strategic policies and business plans yielding the desired results, achievement of budget targets and key performance indicators, improving company's balance sheet and shareholders' value, adoption of best practices of good corporate governance, Corporate Social Responsibility initiatives, enhancing company's goodwill and image, and other indicators. The Board may engage an external consultant to conduct boardroom review/Board evaluation. The methodology includes one-on-one interviews and observation of a Board meeting to provide an independent external view of the Board's effectiveness. The report may identify the areas where enhancement is needed and should be considered. Additionally, evaluation of effectiveness of Board Audit, Finance, HR and other committees may also be undertaken for value addition.

BOARD'S ROLE IN RISK ASSESSMENT AND MANAGEMENT

Companies and businesses face risks on a regular basis and without assuming calculated risks, the progress and success of a company are not possible. However, a system must be built that ensures that core business operations are safeguarded against key risks and threats arising out of internal factors and the external operating environment. The Board is responsible for ensuring that all risks facing the business, assets (tangible and intangible), HR and other resources and intellectual rights of the company are properly identified, assessed and evaluated, managed and mitigated. In the absence of such a risk assessment and management system, all efforts and actions in the company will be an exercise in futility and the company's resources will go down the drain. The Board, in order to play its role effectively in developing and enforcing a system of risk assessment and mitigating actions, constitutes a 'Board Risk Assessment and Management Committee' (RA&MC). The Board, while deciding the committee's membership, needs to consider that the members have broad commercial knowledge, extensive business leadership skills, a broad and suitable mix of business and financial experience and have held various roles in major business, treasury and financial function supervision. Terms of Reference (ToR) of the committee should be finalized, clearly defining the role, responsibility and authority. Access to record and premises should be ensured and adequate technical and manpower resources and management support provided to help the committee discharge its responsibility effectively.

The first step to develop a Risk Assessment and Management model is to identify all potential risks facing the company. Whereas the nature and degree of risk varies from company to company, business to business, country to country and region to region, there are certain common risks such as safety, terrorism, demand and supply pattern, unstable plant operations, natural calamities, climate change, loss of trained and high potential employees, non-compliance with the company's values and standards of governance, fraudulent and unethical practices, law and order situation, exchange/ interest rate, economic and political instability, and other risks.

The next step in the risk assessment process is to define the Risk (Audit) universe, which is a fundamental requirement for risk ranking. This is a comprehensive exercise covering all activities across the company. It is normally entrusted to a dedicated team of Internal Audit (IA) and is primarily based on knowledge and understanding of the company's operations and strategic plan, organizational structure and functional responsibilities, and statements and interviews with responsible management personnel.

The RA&M committee shall guide and supervise the process with practical involvement on a random basis. The committee, in consultation with management, will decide on 'risk appetite' level, which determines the amount of risk the company can accept. The Risk Assessment model will identify the risk factors and assign a value to each risk factor on the basis of the above study. Each activity in the audit universe shall be rated on its risk factors and accordingly placed in High Risk, Medium Risk, or Low Risk categories. On the basis of risk rating and categorization, the committee will identify the areas and activities that require focused risk coverage measures, a vigilant monitoring mechanism, and timely corrective and accountability actions. This will obviously translate into resource allocation to the internal audit team and will also set priorities for the RA&M committee's intervention and focus.

After placing the systems, verification and monitoring mechanism, and accountability processes in place and providing an enabling environment, the committee should focus on delivery strategy. A regular interaction with the management team, surprise visits to the company's sites and installations and interviews with operational staff on a random basis, close liaison with the internal audit team, external auditors and Board Audit Committee to share and exchange views and reports on risk related issues will help achieve the objective. The committee schedules its meetings on a regular basis and considers the reports and updates of the supporting teams and observations of committee members. Presentations are made on various assignments by the respective team head. The committee sets its principal focus on smooth working of systems and controls managing and mitigating key risks. During the review process, weaknesses in certain systems and control mechanisms may be noticed and the committee may identify the areas and functions that need to undergo a fresh risk assessment process on the basis of reports and findings and/or recent internal/external developments. The committee accordingly decides to switch over or allocate additional manpower, IT and other resources to the respective areas and this would be an ongoing process. The committee normally prepares and presents its reports to the Board on quarterly basis, highlighting a summary of reports and findings and recommendations to sustain and improve the risk-governing environment in the company with main emphasis on high risk areas.

The Board, in its position as the supreme governing body of the company, should view the risk management policy as an integral component of the company's strategy aimed at creating, protecting and enhancing shareholders' value by managing the uncertainties, risks and threats that could influence the achievement of corporate goals and objectives. With this mindset, the Board should assign priority and importance to the function of risk management in the company and carefully and extensively review the reports and recommendations of the Committee and extend full support and resource backup.

The Board, in order to have an independent overview of the risk management function, may discuss the issue with the internal audit and control team, internal and external auditors, and Board Audit Committee. The Board may further engage a professional external consultant to review and report on the effectiveness of the risk management function in the company, identify any weaknesses in the control environment and suggest mitigating measures.

BOARD'S ROLE IN STRATEGY AND RISK TO CORPORATE RESPONSIBILITY

Every company must act as a responsible corporate citizen and fulfil all of its corporate responsibilities in letter and spirit. The Board plays a pivotal and decisive role in the company, meeting its corporate obligations alongside its corporate objectives. The Board must realize that it is not only an ongoing compliance process but must also continually match any and all amendments in corporate and financial legislation and applicability of accounting, audit, reporting and other standards. The Board, as the first step to strategy design, may identify and list the corporate responsibilities under all applicable statutes, rules, regulations, codes and standards. The list may include—but not be limited to—the following:

1. Board composition with required number of independent, non-executive, executive and minority directors, election of directors, filling up casual vacancies, filing statutory returns with SECP, stock exchanges and web placement.
2. Holding Board and shareholders' meetings in a timely manner observing notice period, quorum, and other legal requirements. Circulation of minutes and dissemination of Board's decisions in line with disclosure requirement, delegation of powers, and approving statutory appointments.
3. Maintenance of all statutory registers and books of account and preparation, audit, finalization, approval, dissemination, dispatch and web placement of financial statements of the company.
4. Meeting company's obligations on any loan and other dues to a bank or financial institution and redemption/repayment of TFCs, *sukuk*, or any other debt instrument. Covenants attached to any loan/financing facility must also be continually observed.
5. Progress on key litigation cases filed against the company, labour issues, major capital expenditure projects, key contracts and company's obligations thereof and milestone dates/payments should be closely observed.
6. Adequate return on shareholders' investment, recommending dividend in proportion to profit earned

by the company and principal/profit payment on TFCs, *sukuks,* and any other debt instrument to be ensured.

7. Company's ability to continue as a going concern, sustainability report, CSR initiatives, and international quality standards to be observed.

The Board will address the risk to corporate responsibility of the company as an integral part of the Risk Management Policy of the company and will ensure continual compliance through regular review and verification processes.

Chapter 6

Focusing on Financial Stewardship and Accountability

S. Masoud Ali Naqvi

FOCUS ON CORPORATE GOVERNANCE—BOARD OVERSIGHT

Corporate governance principles, practices, and code have been gaining more and more importance and were being developed in most jurisdictions over the years since the early 1960s. The US took the lead by initiating the process through Managerial Capitalism in the 1960s–1970s, moving to Investors Capitalism in the 1980s, during which period the market for corporate control moved from weak to strong and medium level, with Insider's 'Advising Board', weak regulators, and relatively less complex accounting standards. The scenario changed in the 1990s and 2000s to Outsiders' Monitoring Board with stronger regulations. However, the increasing corporate failures in the late 1990s and early 2000s led to regulatory activism and the Sarbanes-Oxley Act, 2002 was introduced with the following five main objectives:

- To strengthen the independence of auditing firms

- To improve the quality and transparency of financial statements and corporate disclosure
- To enhance corporate governance
- To improve the objectivity of research
- To strengthen the enforcement of Federal Securities law, including the use of criminal penalties.

In the UK, the importance of corporate governance was identified in the early 1990s, which resulted in the Cadbury Report in 1992. The Cadbury Report was followed by the Greenberry Report in 1995, the Hamples Report in 1998, the Combined Code in 1998, and the Turnbull Report in 1999. In 2003, the Higgs and Smith Reports were issued, following the UK Directors Remuneration Report Regulations. The Combined Code was revised several times and in 2010 was renamed as the UK Corporate Governance Code.

In 1990, the Organisation for Economic Cooperation and Development (OECD) released the OECD Principles of Corporate Governance, which were later revised; the Revised Principles were released in 2004. These principles were generally considered the model for a number of other jurisdictions. The draft of further Revised OECD Principles was released in November 2014 for public comments up to January 2015. The revised principles were based on various studies of the financial crisis and its impact. The 75 comments received on the revised draft are being analysed and the revised text is scheduled for completion soon.

The corporate governance principles and codes developed in a number of jurisdictions have all focused on

'Qualified Board Oversight' and relevant risk management of the overall affairs of a corporate entity, including financial oversight. The analysts of the financial crisis, therefore, to a great extent attributed the crisis to failure and weaknesses in corporate governance arrangements and a key conclusion was that 'Qualified Board Oversight' and 'Robust Risk Management' are important and require continuous review to deal with an evolving complex commerce and business environment.

In Pakistan, the first Code was issued in 2002, which was a significant move forward to achieve improvement in quality of the Boards, ethical compliance, independence, and reiteration of the role assigned to the Board under the statutes and laws applicable to the corporate sector (listed companies). The review of the Code in 2012 was based on the experience of the implementation of the earlier Code and the focus was to ensure the independence, integrity and quality of the leadership provided by the Board. 'The Board should be able to exercise objective, independent judgment on corporate affairs' (OECD Principles).

The competence and capability of directors should also get due importance. The Board members should have suitable qualification and at a minimum clear a fit and proper test, but the focus should be on ensuring that directors have adequate knowledge of business, acquire appropriate skills upon appointment and thereafter remain abreast of relevant laws, regulations and changing risks through in-house training and external courses. A strong Board is one that has Board members who have a high level of integrity, an independent mindset, and are knowledgeable about the business environment, risks profiles and challenges. However, passive Boards are very common, where a majority of Board members generally have an inadequate understanding of business and are weak on inclusion.

In terms of financial oversight, the role of the Board is generally performed through an Audit Committee, which is a Board Committee.

The Audit Committee in the performance of its role and providing comfort or otherwise to the Board is required to be actively engaged with the Internal Audit function of the Company, and the Committee can engage outside experts if it deems necessary for obtaining the satisfaction that would enable it to recommend or present to the Board all financial, risk management and other relevant matters.

In order to ensure that an Audit Committee does perform its function and role effectively with close interaction with Financial Management, Internal Audit, and External Auditors, it is vital to have focused training on an ongoing basis to enable the Committee to support the Board in its financial oversight role. The role of the Audit Committee as specified in the Code of Corporate Governance 2012 is given later. The members of the Audit Committee and the Board are to be provided access to all financial and other relevant information to enable them to make appropriate and informed decisions/recommendations.

REPORTING: THE REPORTING ENVIRONMENT AND LEGAL OBLIGATIONS FOR EFFECTIVE STAKEHOLDER COMMUNICATIONS

Reporting Environment

The term stakeholder means any person or group that can affect or be affected by the policies or activities of an organization.

The need for transparency and disclosures in the financial markets is recognized in codes and statements of principles on corporate governance.

- The UK Corporate Governance Code (Combined Code) includes a principle about the disclosure of financial information by companies, stating that the Board has the responsibility to present 'a balanced and understandable assessment' of the company's position and prospects in its financial reporting.
- The OECD Principles state the requirement with greater force. These state that companies should provide 'timely and accurate disclosure' about their financial performance and position, and also about the ownership of shares in the company and other corporate governance issues.
- The International Corporate Governance Network (ICGN) Principles emphasize the need for information so that investors can make investment decisions. They state that companies should, on a timely basis, disclose

the relevant information about the company to enable informed decisions to be made by investors about the acquisition, obligations and rights, ownership and sale of shares.

There are several basic principles for disclosure and communication of information:

- The information should be reliable. Reliable information is information that is sufficiently accurate for investors to trust it when making their investment decisions. The OECD Principles, for example, state that information should be prepared and disclosed with high quality standards of accounting and high standards for both financial and non-financial disclosures.
- Information should be understandable. One of the criticisms of International Financial Reporting Standards (IFRSs) is that financial reporting in accordance with IFRSs can be very complex, and some investors might not properly understand the information that they provide. Many investors support the idea that companies should provide information in a narrative form, in addition to providing financial statements.
- Information should be timely. In the financial markets, 'timely' often means 'communicated as soon as possible'. Information should be made available to all investors as soon as possible after it becomes 'public'. Efficient stock markets should ensure that information announced by companies is made available to everyone quickly after the announcement. In the European Union, for

example, one of the aims of the Transparency Directive (introduced in 2007) is to communicate information available quickly to investors as soon as companies make announcements to the stock market.

- When information is disclosed by companies, it should be equally available to all investors. The OECD Principles state that the way information is distributed should enable users to access the relevant information in an equal, timely, and cost-efficient manner.
- Information should be made available by convenient channels of communication. Companies should be encouraged to make it available in electronic form to investors who want to receive it in that form. For example, companies should use their websites for making disclosures.
- The opportunities for exploiting confidential information to make a personal profit should be minimized and by making information available to investors quickly, opportunities for insider trading should be reduced.

REGULATORY REQUIREMENTS—PAKISTAN

Audit and Financial Reporting Requirement for Listed Companies

Listed public companies are required to circulate to shareholders quarterly and annual financial statements. They are also required to file copies with the Stock Exchanges and SECP. The quarterly reports for the first and third quarter must be circulated/filed within one month of the close of the quarter and annual reports are due within four months of the financial year-end. Second quarter reports are due within two months of the end of the quarter. The SECP may, for good reason, grant an extension of up to two months for submitting annual reports.

The mandated financial year-end is September 30th for manufacturers of sugar. The financial year-end for banks and insurance companies is December 31st. All other companies must have a financial year-end of June 30th, unless an exemption is obtained from the Federal Board of Revenue.

Annual financial statements, together with information regarding shareholders and directors, must be filed with the Registrar of Joint Stock Companies within 45 days of the annual shareholders' meeting. The annual financial statements must be audited and second quarter financial statements must be reviewed by auditors.

Directors' report to the shareholders on the company's state of affairs, recommendations for dividend, and other matters should be attached to the financial statements. A report on status of compliance with the Code of Corporate Governance must accompany annual financial statements and such status should be reviewed by the auditors.

Listed public companies are also required to submit a statement showing the pattern of shareholdings at the date of the annual financial statements. Reports must be in English. Companies with subsidiaries are also required to publish consolidated financial statements. Printed reports are made available, without exception, to all shareholders, banks, financial institutions, government agencies and the financial press. Companies may avail the option of putting their financial statements on the web after obtaining shareholders' approval in an annual general meeting.

Every company is required to keep proper accounting records with respect to all sums of money received or expended by the company, all purchases and sales by the company, and assets and liabilities of the company. Waiver of reporting requirements are available upon application to the SECP, when a company can prove that reporting certain information is either impractical or not in its interest.

Audit and Financial Reporting Requirements for Public Unlisted and Private Companies

Annual financial statements must be presented at the annual shareholders' meeting, which in the case of new companies must be held within 18 months of incorporation. Thereafter, the annual meeting must be held at least once in a calendar year, but the time gap between the meetings must not exceed 15 months.

Furthermore, the financial statements presented at the meeting must not be more than four months old. The Registrar of Joint Stock Companies may, for good reason, extend the four-month period by a further period not to exceed two months.

Public unlisted companies are required to file a copy of the financial statements contained in the reports with the

Registrar, together with information regarding shareholders and directors within 30 days of the annual meeting.

The financial statements are the same as for listed public companies, except that quarterly information is not required. The statements must be audited. A person other than a chartered accountant can also be appointed auditor of a private company, if it is not a subsidiary of a public company. The reports are made available to the shareholders and, where necessary, to banks, financial institutions and government agencies. They need not be published. Other reporting requirements are generally the same as for listed public companies.

Audit and Financial Reporting Requirements for Banks

Annual financial statements should comply with the Banking Companies Ordinance, 1962, and must be filed annually with the State Bank of Pakistan by March 31st. The mandated financial year-end is December 31st. The State Bank of Pakistan may, under special circumstances, extend the due date by a period up to three months.

Banks are required to publish their annual and quarterly (except for the fourth quarter) financial statements in the national press and display them at each branch office. The financial statements for the second quarter must be reviewed by the auditors. Other requirements, where applicable, for banks regarding language of reports, consolidated financial statements, directors' report, availability of printed reports and accounting records are the same as for listed public companies.

REGULATORY REQUIREMENTS

Following the legal requirements of Pakistan ensures effective stakeholders communication:

- Section 158(1) of the Companies Ordinance 1984 states: 'Every company shall hold, in addition to any other meeting, a general meeting, as its annual general meeting, within eighteen months from the date of its incorporation and thereafter once at least in every calendar year within a period of four months following the close of its financial year and not more than fifteen months after the holding of its last preceding annual general meeting.'
- Section 158(3) of the Companies Ordinance 1984 states: 'The notice of an annual general meeting shall be sent to the shareholders at least twenty-one days before the date fixed for the meeting and, in the case of a listed company, such notice, in addition to its being dispatched in the normal course, shall also be published at least in one issue each of a daily newspaper in English language and a daily newspaper in Urdu language having circulation in the Province in which the stock exchange on which the company is listed is situate.'
- Section 159(1) of the Companies Ordinance 1984 states: 'All general meetings of a company, other than

the annual general meeting referred to in section 158 and the statutory meeting mentioned in section 157, shall be called extraordinary general meetings.'

- Section 159(2) of the Companies Ordinance 1984 states: 'The directors may at any time call an extraordinary general meeting of the company to consider any matter which requires the approval of the company in a general meeting, and shall, on the requisition of members representing not less than one-tenth of the voting powers on the date of the deposit of the requisition, forthwith proceed to call an extraordinary general meeting.'
- Section 236 of the Companies Ordinance 1984 states: 'The directors shall make out and attach to every balance sheet a report with respect to the state of the company's affairs, the amount, if any, which they recommend should be paid by way of dividend and the amount, if any, which they propose to carry to the Reserve Fund, General Reserve or Reserve Account shown specifically in the balance sheet or to a Reserve Fund, General Reserve or Reserve Account to be shown specifically in a subsequent balance sheet.'
- Section xvi of the Code of Corporate Governance 2012 states: 'The directors of listed companies shall annex statements to the following effect with the Directors' Report, prepared under Section 236 of the Ordinance:

    1. The financial statements, prepared by the management of the listed company, present its state of affairs fairly, the result of its operations, cash flows and changes in equity;

2. Proper books of account of the listed company have been maintained;
3. Appropriate accounting policies have been consistently applied in preparation of financial statements and accounting estimates are based on reasonable and prudent judgment;
4. International Financial Reporting Standards, as applicable in Pakistan, have been followed in preparation of financial statements and any departure therefrom has been adequately disclosed and explained;
5. The system of internal control is sound in design and has been effectively implemented and monitored; and
6. There are no significant doubts upon the listed company's ability to continue as a going concern.

Provided that where necessary the following information shall also be annexed to the Directors' Reports of listed companies:

- If the listed company is not considered to be a going concern, the fact along with the reasons shall be disclosed;
- Significant deviations from last year in operating results of the listed company shall be highlighted and reasons thereof shall be explained;
- Key operating and financial data of the last six years shall be summarized;
- If the listed company has neither declared dividend nor

issued bonus shares for any year, the reasons thereof shall be given;

- Where any statutory payment on account of taxes, duties, levies and charges is outstanding, the amount together with a brief description and reasons for the same shall be disclosed;
- Significant plans and decisions, such as corporate restructuring, business expansion and discontinuance of operations, shall be outlined along with future prospects, risks and uncertainties surrounding the listed company;
- A statement as to the value of investments of provident, gratuity and pension funds, based on their respective audited accounts, shall be included;
- The number of board and committees' meetings held during the year and attendance by each director shall be disclosed;
- The details of training programmes attended by directors;
- The pattern of shareholding shall be reported to disclose the aggregate number of shares (along with name wise details where stated below) held by:

  – associated companies, undertakings and related parties (name wise details);
  – mutual funds (name wise details);
  – directors and their spouse(s) and minor children (name wise details);
  – executives;
  – public sector companies and corporations;
  – banks, development finance institutions, non-banking

finance companies, insurance companies, *takaful*, *modarabas* and pension funds; and

- shareholders holding five per cent or more voting rights in the listed company (name wise details).
  Explanation: For the purpose of this sub-clause, the expression 'executive' means an employee of a listed company other than the CEO and directors.

- The directors' report shall cover loans, TFCs, *sukuks*, or any other debt instruments in which the company is in default or likely to default. There shall be a clear presentation with details as to the aggregate amount of the debt overdue or likely to become overdue, the reasons for the default/emerging default situation and the measures taken by the company to address and settle such default situation.
- All trades in the shares of the listed company carried out by its directors, executives and their spouses and minor children shall also be disclosed. Explanation: For the purpose of this sub-clause and clause xxiii the expression 'executive' means the CEO, COO, CFO, Head of Internal Audit and Company Secretary by whatever name called, and other employees of the company for whom the board of directors will set the threshold to be reviewed on an annual basis and disclosed in the annual report.

CORPORATE FINANCE: KEY ELEMENTS IN DETERMINING A COMPANY'S CAPITAL GEARING, DIVIDEND POLICY AND VALUATION

Key Elements in Determining a Company's Capital Gearing

The following factors are considered in determining a company's capital gearing:

- **Trading on Equity:** The word 'equity' denotes the ownership of the company. Trading on equity means taking advantage of equity share capital to borrow funds on a reasonable basis. It refers to additional profits that equity shareholders earn because of issuance of debentures/bonds and preference shares. It is based on the thought that if the rate of dividend on preference capital and the rate of interest on borrowed capital is lower than the general rate of the company's earnings, equity shareholders are at an advantage, which means a company should go for a judicious blend of preference shares, equity shares, as well as debentures. Trading on equity becomes more important when the expectations of shareholders are high.

- **Degree of Control:** Directors of companies have got greater rights as compared to preference shareholders and debenture holders. Preference shareholders have less voting rights while debenture holders have no voting rights. If the company's management policies are such that they want to retain their voting rights in their hands, the capital structure consists of debenture holders and loans rather than equity shares.

- **Flexibility of Financial Plan:** In an enterprise, the capital structure should be such that there are both contractions as well as relaxation in plans. Debentures and loans can be refunded as and when the time requires, while equity capital cannot be refunded at any point, which provides rigidity to plans. Therefore, in order to make the capital structure flexible, the company should go for an issue of debentures and other loans.

- **Choice of Investors:** A company's policy generally is to have different categories of investors for securities. Therefore, a capital structure should give enough choice to all kind of investors to invest. Bold and adventurous investors generally go for equity shares and loans and debentures are generally raised keeping in mind conscious investors.

- **Capital Market Condition:** In the lifetime of the company, the market price of the shares has an important influence. During a depression period, the company's capital structure generally consists of debentures and loans while in periods of a boom, the company's capital should consist of share capital, generally equity shares.

- **Period of Financing:** When a company wants to raise finance for a short period, it goes for loans from banks and other institutions, while for a long period it goes for the issue of shares and debentures.

- **Cost of Financing:** In the capital structure, the company has to look to the factor of cost when securities are raised. It is seen that debentures at a time of profit earning of the company prove to be a cheaper source of finance as compared to equity shares where equity shareholders demand an extra share in profits.

- **Stability of Sales:** An established business that has a growing market and high sales turnover is in a position to meet fixed commitments. Interest on debentures has to be paid regardless of profit. Therefore, when sales are high, the profits are high, and the company is in a better position to meet such fixed commitments as interest on debentures and dividends on preference shares. If the company is suffering unstable sales, then it is not in a position to meet fixed obligations. Equity capital proves to be safer in such circumstances.

- **Size of a Company:** A small size business firm's capital structure generally consists of loans from banks and retained profits while on the other hand, big companies having goodwill, stability and an established profit can easily go for issuance of shares and debentures as well as loans and borrowings from financial institutions. The bigger the size, the wider the total capitalization.

- **Company's Tax Exposure:** Debt payments are tax deductible. As such, if a company's tax rate is high, using debt as a means of financing a project is attractive because the tax deductibility of the debt payments protects some income from taxes.

- **Management Style:** Management styles range from aggressive to conservative. The more conservative a management's approach is, the less inclined it is to use debt to increase profits. An aggressive management may try to grow the firm quickly, using significant amounts of debt to ramp up the growth of the company's earnings per share.

- **Growth Rate:** Firms that are in the growth stage of their cycle typically finance that growth through debt by borrowing money to grow faster. The conflict that arises with this method is that the revenues of growth firms are typically unstable and unproven. As such, a high debt load is usually not appropriate.

  More stable and mature firms typically need less debt to finance growth as their revenues are stable and proven. These firms also generate cash flow, which can be used to finance projects when they arise.

Key Elements in Determining a Company's Dividend Policy

The following factors are considered in determining a company's dividend policy:

- **Type of Industry:** Industries that are characterized by stability of earnings may formulate a more consistent policy as to dividends than those having an uneven flow of income. For example, public utilities concerns are in a much better position to adopt a relatively fixed dividend rate than industrial concerns.

- **Age of Corporation:** Newly established enterprises require most of their earnings for plant improvement and expansion, while older companies that have attained a longer earning experience can formulate clear cut dividend policies and may even be liberal in the distribution of dividends.

- **Extent of Share Distribution:** A closely held company is likely to get the consent of the shareholders for the suspension of dividends or for following a conservative dividend policy. But a company with a large number of shareholders widely scattered would face great difficulty in securing such assent. Reduction in dividends can be effected but not without the cooperation of shareholders.

- **Need for Additional Capital:** The extent to which profits are ploughed back into the business has a considerable influence on the dividend policy. The income may be conserved for meeting the increased requirements of working capital or future expansion.

- **Business Cycles:** During a boom, prudent corporate management create good reserves for facing the crisis that follows an inflationary period. Higher rates of dividend are used as a tool for marketing the securities in an otherwise depressed market.

- **Changes in Government Policies:** Sometimes governments limit the rate of dividend declared by companies in a particular industry or in all spheres of business activity.

- **Trends of Profits:** The past trend of the company's profits should be thoroughly examined to find out the average earning position of the company. The average earnings should be subjected to the trends of general economic conditions. If a depression is approaching, only a conservative dividend policy can be regarded as prudent.

- **Future Requirements:** Accumulation of profits becomes necessary to provide against contingencies (or hazards) of the business, to finance future expansion of the business and to modernize or replace equipment of the enterprise. The conflicting claims of dividends and accumulation should be equitably settled by the management.

- **Cash Balance:** If the working capital of the company is small, a liberal policy of cash dividends cannot be adopted. Dividends then have to take the form of bonus shares issued to the members in lieu of cash payment.

Key Elements in Determining a Company's Valuation

The most commonly used and generally accepted techniques of valuing companies are as follows:

- Discounted cash flows (DCF) method
- Adjusted Net Asset Value (NAV) Method
- Comparable Companies/Transactions-based Multiples Method

DCF Method

DCF is the most commonly used valuation technique. It implies a value for the business by calculating the present value of a future stream of cash flows.

The DCF method utilizes financial projections of a business to determine future free cash flows of the company. The financial projections are generally prepared for a minimum period of five years. The projected free cash flows are then discounted to their present value using the company's Weighted Average Cost of Capital (WACC). A terminal value at the end of the explicit forecast period is then determined and that value is also discounted back to the valuation date to give an overall value for the business.

This method is heavily dependent on cash flows and growth characteristics, and can be applied when the company has positive projected cash flows.

Adjusted NAV Method

This method seeks to overcome the shortcomings that appear when purely accounting criteria are applied in the valuation.

Under this method, the book values of the assets and liabilities of a company are matched to market value in order to arrive at their fair-market value and any unrecorded assets and liabilities are also identified in order to arrive at the adjusted NAV.

Adjusted NAV method is most applicable for businesses where the value lies in the underlying assets.

Comparable Companies/Transactions-based Multiples Method

This method is based on the assumption that similar assets sell at similar prices. It assumes that a ratio or multiple comparing values to some firm-specific variable (earnings, sales, cash flows, etc.) is the same across similar firms or transactions in which similar companies have been engaged.

Multiples of similar publicly traded companies or publicly announced transactions in respect of similar companies are applied to the company being valued in order to calculate the derived value.

The reliability of this technique depends on the level of comparability of the selected companies or transactions. This method is also used to provide a market cross-check to the conclusions reached under a DCF approach.

INTERNAL CONTROLS

The Basel Committee on Banking Supervision, 1998, stated the following principles for an effective internal control system:

Principal 4: An effective internal control system requires that the material risks that could adversely affect the achievement of the bank's goals are being recognized and continually assessed. This assessment should cover all risks facing the bank and the consolidated banking organization (that is, credit risk, country and transfer risk, market risk, interest rate risk, liquidity risk, operational risk, legal risk and reputational risk). Internal controls may need to be revised to appropriately address any new or previously uncontrolled risks.

Principal 5: Control activities should be an integral part of the daily activities of a bank. An effective internal control system requires that an appropriate control structure is set up, with control activities defined at every business level. These should include: top level reviews; appropriate activity controls for different departments or divisions; physical controls; checking for compliance with exposure limits and follow-up on non-compliance; a system of approvals and authorizations and a system of verification and reconciliation.

Principal 6: An effective internal control system requires that there is appropriate segregation of duties and personnel are not assigned conflicting responsibilities. Areas of potential conflicts of interest should be identified, minimized, and subjected to careful, independent monitoring.

Principal 7: An effective internal control system requires that there are adequate and comprehensive internal financial, operational and compliance data, as well as external market information about events and conditions that are relevant to decision making. Information should be reliable, timely, accessible, and provided in a consistent format.

Principal 8: An effective internal control system requires that there are reliable information systems in place that cover all significant activities of the bank. These systems, including those that hold and use data in an electronic form, must be secure, monitored independently and supported by adequate contingency arrangements.

Principal 9: An effective internal control system requires effective channels of communication to ensure that all staff fully understand and adhere to policies and procedures affecting their duties and responsibilities and that other relevant information is reaching the appropriate personnel.

REQUIREMENTS OF CODE OF CORPORATE GOVERNANCE, 2012 (AMENDED IN JULY, 2014)

- As per section VD, the Board of Directors of a listed company shall ensure that 'a system of sound internal control is established, which is effectively implemented and maintained at all levels within the company.'
- As per section ix, '... internal audit reports, including cases of fraud, bribery, corruption, or irregularities of a material nature ...' should be placed for decision before the Board of Directors.
- As per section xxxi, 'There shall be an internal audit function in every listed company. The Head of internal Audit shall functionally report to the Audit Committee and administratively to the CEO.

  A director cannot be appointed, in any capacity, in the internal audit function, to ensure independence of the internal audit function.

  The internal audit function may be outsourced by a listed company to a professional services firm or be performed by the internal audit staff of holding company. However, due care shall be exercised to ensure that suitably qualified and experienced persons, who are conversant with the company's policies and procedures, are engaged in the internal audit. In the event of outsourcing the internal audit function, company shall appoint or designate a fulltime employee other than CFO, as Head of Internal Audit, to act as coordinator between firm providing internal audit services and the Board:

Provided that while outsourcing the function, the company must not appoint its existing external auditors as internal auditors.'

- As per section xxxii, 'All listed companies shall ensure that internal audit reports are provided for the review of external auditors. The auditors shall discuss any major findings in relation to the reports with the Audit Committee, which shall report matters of significance to the Board of Directors.'

ROLE OF AUDIT COMMITTEE

The audit committee is a committee of the Board of Directors consisting of at least three members comprising non-executive directors and at least one independent director. The chairman of the committee shall preferably be an independent director, who shall not be the Chairman of the Board. The Board shall satisfy itself that at least one member of the audit committee has relevant financial skills/expertise and experience (Code of Corporate Governance, 2014).

Following are the roles of the Audit Committee:

As per Code of Corporate Governance 2012, amended in July 2014:

- Determination of appropriate measures to safeguard the listed company's assets;
- Review of quarterly, half-yearly and annual financial

statements of the listed company, prior to their approval by the Board of Directors, focusing on:

- major judgemental areas;
- significant adjustments resulting from the audit;
- the going concern assumption;
- any changes in accounting policies and practices;
- compliance with applicable accounting standards;
- compliance with listing regulations and other statutory and regulatory requirements, and
- significant related party transactions.

- Review of preliminary announcements of results prior to publication;
- Facilitating the external audit and discussion with external auditors of major observations arising from interim and final audits and any matter that the auditors may wish to highlight (in the absence of management, where necessary);
- Review of management letter issued by external auditors and management's response thereto;
- Ensuring coordination between the internal and external auditors of the listed company;
- Review of the scope and extent of internal audit and ensuring that the internal audit function has adequate resources and is appropriately placed within the listed company;
- Consideration of major findings of internal investigations of activities characterized by fraud, corruption and abuse of power and management's response thereto;
- Ascertaining that the internal control systems including financial and operational controls, accounting systems

for timely and appropriate recording of purchases and sales, receipts and payments, assets and liabilities and the reporting structure are adequate and effective;

- Review of the listed company's statement on internal control systems prior to endorsement by the Board of Directors and internal audit reports;
- Instituting special projects, value for money studies or other investigations on any matter specified by the Board of Directors, in consultation with the CEO, and to consider remittance of any matter to the external auditors or to any other external body;
- Determination of compliance with relevant statutory requirements;
- Monitoring compliance with the best practices of corporate governance and identification of significant violations thereof, and
- Consideration of any other issue or matter as may be assigned by the Board of Directors.
- The Audit Committee of a listed company shall appoint a secretary of the committee who shall either be the Company Secretary or Head of Internal Audit. However, the CFO shall not be appointed as the secretary of the Audit Committee. The secretary shall circulate minutes of meetings of the Audit Committee to all members, directors, Head of Internal Audit and the CFO prior to the next meeting of the Board and where this is not practicable, the Chairman of the Audit Committee shall communicate a synopsis of the proceedings to the Board and the minutes shall be circulated immediately after the meeting of the Board.

- The Head of Internal Audit shall functionally report to the Audit Committee and administratively to the CEO.
- The external auditors shall discuss any major findings in relation to the reports with the Audit Committee, which shall report matters of significance to the Board of Directors.
- The Board of Directors of a listed company shall recommend appointment of external auditors for a year, as suggested by the Audit Committee.
- The details of all related party transactions shall be placed before the Audit Committee of the company and upon recommendations of the Audit Committee the same shall be placed before the Board for review and approval.
- The related party transactions that are not executed at arm's length price shall also be placed separately at each Board meeting along with necessary justification for consideration and approval of the Board on recommendation of the Audit Committee of the listed company.
- The removal of Head of Internal Audit shall be made with the approval of the Board only upon recommendation of the Chairman of the Audit Committee.
- It shall be mandatory for the CEO and CFO to have the second quarterly and annual accounts (both separate and consolidated where applicable) initialled by the external auditors before presenting them to the Audit Committee and the Board of Directors for approval.
- The Audit Committee shall meet the external auditors

without the CFO and the Head of Internal Audit being present:

- Provided further that at least once a year, the Audit Committee shall meet the Head of Internal Audit and other members of the internal audit function without the CFO and the external auditors being present:
- Provided further that the chairman of the Audit Committee and engagement partner of the external auditor or in his absence any other partner designated by the audit firm shall be present at the Annual General Meeting for necessary feedback to the shareholders.

As per SBP's Handbook of Corporate Governance

- Determination of appropriate measures to safeguard the bank's assets.
- Review of preliminary announcements of results prior to publication.
- Review of quarterly, half-yearly and annual financial statements, prior to their approval by the Board of Directors, focusing on:
  - major judgemental areas;
  - significant adjustments resulting from the audit;
  - the going-concern assumption;
  - any changes in accounting policies and practices;
  - Compliance with applicable accounting standards;
  - Compliance with listing regulations and other statutory and regulatory requirements.

- Facilitating the external audit and discussion with external auditors of major observations arising from interim and final audits and any matter that the auditors may wish to highlight (in the absence of management, where necessary).
- Review of management letter issued by external auditors and management's response thereto.
- Ensuring coordination between the internal and external auditors.
- Review of the scope and extent of internal audit and ensuring that the internal audit function has adequate resources and is appropriately placed within the bank.
- Consideration of major findings of internal investigations and management's response thereto.
- Ascertaining that the internal control system including financial and operational controls, accounting system and reporting structure are adequate and effective.
- Review of the statement on internal control systems prior to endorsement by the Board of Directors.
- Instituting special projects, value for money studies or other investigations on any matter specified by the Board of Directors, in consultation with the chief executive, and to consider remittance of any matter to the external auditors or to any other external body.
- Determination of compliance with relevant statutory requirements.
- Monitoring compliance with the best practices of corporate governance and identification of significant violations thereof.

- Consideration of any other issue or matter as may be assigned by the Board of Directors.

As per the Basel Committee Principles on Bank's Internal Controls

Principle 19

- Audit Committee assists Board of Directors' task to ensure the existence and maintenance of adequate system of internal controls.
- Audit Committee reinforces internal control system, internal and external audits.
- Audit Committee should have a proper written charter.
- Audit Committee should have at least three members of the Board who are not current or former members of senior management.
- Audit Committee should have at least one member having a background in financial reporting, accounting or auditing.
- Audit Committee should approve ('confirm') the internal audit charter, the audit plan and the resources required.

As per UK Combined Code of Corporate Governance

- To monitor integrity of the financial statements.

- To review the company's internal financial controls (and its risk management systems).
- To monitor and review the effectiveness of internal audit.
- To recommend (to the Board) appointment of the external auditors and approve their remuneration and terms of engagement.
- To review and monitor the external auditor's independence, objectivity and the effectiveness of the audit process.
- To develop and implement policy on using the external auditor to render non-audit services.
- To institute whistle-blowing arrangements.

EXTERNAL AUDIT REQUIREMENTS

Cadbury (1992) declared that 'the annual audit is one of the cornerstones of corporate governance ... The audit provides an external and objective check on the way in which the financial statements have been prepared and presented ...' Through the role of the external auditor, the shareholders monitor and control the management and this helps to enhance transparency in a company.

The qualification, independence and appointment of auditors' requirements are as follow:

Qualification of Auditors

Auditors must be members of the Institute of Chartered

Accountants of Pakistan (ICAP). A firm where all of its partners are members of the ICAP can be appointed as an auditor and act in the firm's name. Private companies may appoint auditors who are not members of the ICAP. In the case of banks, the State Bank of Pakistan has developed a panel of auditors categorizing the firms on the basis of a pre-set criteria as 'A', 'B' and 'C' categories with eligibility to conduct audit of specified banks and DFIs. The auditors of a listed company must also possess a satisfactory quality control rating from the ICAP.

Independence

Independence is required by the Companies Ordinance, 1984. An auditor cannot be a director or officer of the company, be a partner or employee of a director or officer, or be indebted to the company. The firm of external auditors auditing a listed company or any partner in the firm and their spouse and minor children are prohibited to hold, purchase, sell or take any position in shares of the listed company or any of its associated companies or undertakings.

Appointment of Auditors

The first auditors of the company are appointed by the directors of the company within 60 days from the date of incorporation of the company. For subsequent years, the auditors are appointed at each annual general meeting of the company and hold office till the conclusion of the next annual general meeting. Where appointment of auditors is not made at any annual meeting, the Securities and Exchange Commission of Pakistan (SECP) may, upon application of any shareholder of the company, appoint the auditors and fix their remuneration and in the case of casual vacancy, the directors may fill any casual vacancy within 30 days. For public sector companies, two auditors are normally appointed.

The auditors once appointed cannot be removed or changed except in the next annual general meeting. However, a notice proposing the change must be sent by a shareholder to the company at least 14 days before the meeting and the company must communicate this notice to the retiring auditors and give notice to all of its shareholders at least seven days before the meeting. In the case of banks, auditors once appointed should continue for at least three years and in case of any change before completion of three years, banks are required to specify the reason for such change.

Mandatory Rotation of Auditors

The Code of Corporate Governance provides for mandatory rotation of audit firms; in the case of financial sector companies, after every five years, unless exempted by the State Bank of Pakistan. In the case of all other listed companies, the audit partner is required to be rotated after every five years.

Auditing Standards

Members of the ICAP are required to observe the pronouncements of the International Federation of Accountants, as long as these do not conflict with Pakistani laws.

REQUIREMENTS OF COMPANIES ORDINANCE 1984

- As per Section 252 (1): 'Every company shall at each annual general meeting appoint an auditor or auditors to hold office from the conclusion of that meeting until the conclusion of the next annual general meeting.'
- As per Section 252 (3): 'The first auditor or auditors of a company shall be appointed by the directors within sixty days of the date of incorporation of the company; and the auditor or auditors so appointed shall hold office until the conclusion of the first annual general meeting provided that:

  a. the company in a general meeting may remove any such auditor or auditors and appoint in his or their place any other person or persons who have been nominated for appointment by any member of the company and of whose nomination notice has been given to the members of the company not less than fourteen days before the date of the meeting; and
  b. If the directors fail to exercise their powers under

this sub-section, the company in general meeting may appoint the first auditor or auditors.'

REQUIREMENTS OF CODE OF CORPORATE GOVERNANCE 2012, AMENDED IN JULY 2014

- As per section xxviii: 'The CFO, the Head of Internal Audit and external auditors represented by engagement partner or in his absence any other partner designated by the audit firm shall attend meetings of the Audit Committee at which issues relating to accounts and audit are discussed: Provided that at least once a year, the Audit Committee shall meet the external auditors without the CFO and the Head of Internal Audit being present.'
- As per section xxxiii: 'No listed company shall appoint as external auditors a firm of auditors which has not been given a satisfactory rating under the Quality Control Review programme of the Institute of Chartered Accountants of Pakistan.'
- As per section xxxiv: 'No listed company shall appoint as external auditors a firm of auditors which, or a partner of which, is non-compliant with the International Federation of Accountants' (IFAC) Guidelines on Code of Ethics, as adopted by the Institute of Chartered Accountants of Pakistan.'
- As per section xxxv: 'The Board of Directors of a listed company shall recommend appointment of external

auditors for a year, as suggested by the Audit Committee. The recommendations of the Audit Committee for appointment of an auditor or otherwise shall be included in the Directors' Report. In case of a recommendation for appointment of an auditor other than the retiring auditor the reasons for the same shall be included in the Directors' Report.'

- As per section xxxvi: 'No listed company shall appoint its auditors to provide services in addition to audit except in accordance with the regulations and shall require the auditors to observe applicable IFAC guidelines in this regard and shall ensure that the auditors do not perform management functions or make management decisions, responsibility for which remains with the Board of Directors and management of the listed company.'
- As per section xxxvii: '(a) all listed companies in the financial sector shall change their external auditors every five years. Financial sector, for this purpose, means banks, non-banking financial companies (NBFCs), *modarabas* and insurance/*takaful* companies; provided that all interrelated companies/institutions, engaged in business of providing financial services shall appoint the same firm of auditors to conduct the audit of their accounts, and (b) all listed companies other than those in the financial sector shall, at a minimum, rotate the engagement partner after every five years.'
- As per section xxxviii: 'No listed company shall appoint a person as an external auditor or a person involved in the audit of a listed company who is a close relative,

i.e., spouse, parents, dependents and non-dependent children, of the CEO, the CFO, an internal auditor or a director of the listed company.'

- As per section xxxviii: 'Every listed company shall require external auditors to furnish a Management Letter to its board of directors within 45 days of the date of audit report: Provided that any matter deemed significant by the external auditor shall be communicated in writing to the board prior to the approval of the audited accounts by the board.'

CORPORATE GOVERNANCE AND FINANCIAL CRISIS

Triggers (that may affect governance)

- Adverse publicity or criticism: accounting practices, remuneration arrangements or accountability related.
- Criticism of controls, processes, risk management or reporting standards and quality.
- Impending legislation or market pressures that may force changes in reporting requirements.
- Expansion into geographical or business markets that could make the organization subject to new regulations or stakeholders' attention.
- Questions as to whether existing performance measures are appropriate and sufficiently rigorous.
- Technology changes that affect how business operations are carried out.

- Development of new or unanticipated business, industry or market risks.

FINANCIAL CRISIS INDICATORS

The following factors indicate financial crises of a company: Issues of integrity, ethics, propriety and probity.

- Defective HR policies and procedures and high personnel turnover.
- Improper reward and incentive system.
- Lack of qualified personnel at various levels.
- Improper delegation of authority and responsibility.
- Incompatibility in growth and the existing organization and infrastructure.
- Impairing of control processes (preventive and detective) resulting in a higher than reasonable incidence of loss of business, frauds, errors and irregularities.
- Liquidity crises and impaired credit worthiness.
- Shrinking markets denominated by declining business and revenue and squeezing of spreads.
- Threats posed by unfair competition in the market place and changing clients' behaviour.
- Technological threats posed by innovation.
- Litigation and underlying exposure.
- Health, safety and environmental issues.
- Regulatory and compliance exposure.
- Foreign currency risk and exposure.
- Changes in governmental policies (including political

and economic) and legal and regulatory implications arising therefrom.

THE CHALLENGE FOR POLICY MAKERS

The crisis represents a challenge for corporate governance policy.

- The general policy needs are similar for financial and non-financial companies.
- Four aspects of corporate governance require attention:
  - Remuneration/incentive systems
  - Risk management practices
  - The performance of Boards
  - The exercise of shareholder rights.

Remuneration and Incentive Systems: An Old Issue in New Form

- Remuneration and incentive systems need to be considered broadly and not just focused on the CEO and Board members.
- The governance of remuneration/incentive systems have often failed because managers and others had too much influence over the level and conditions for performance-based remuneration.
- In many cases the link between performance and remuneration is very weak or difficult to establish.

- Remuneration schemes are often overly complicated or obscure in ways that camouflage the situation.
- The goals for remuneration/incentive systems need to encourage long term performance.
- The tax system has an important influence on both the level and structure of compensation but whether the outcomes are desirable for the perspective of corporate governance is often far from clear.
- Remuneration should be established through a sound governance process where the roles and responsibilities of those involved are clearly defined and separated.
- It should be considered good practice that remuneration policies are submitted to the annual meeting and are subject to shareholder approval.
- Financial institutions are advised to follow the Principles for Sound Compensation Practices issued by the Financial Stability Forum.

Risk Management Practices and Standards: A Missing Element

- Effective risk management is a key element of good corporate governance. National risk standards are still in a very high level form and may not give good guidance.
- Risk management is important not just in avoiding losses but also in being able to seize new opportunities. Excessive emphasis appears to have been given to financial risk and internal controls for reporting purposes.
- Risk management needs to be an enterprise-wide

undertaking and not just practiced in particular product/market lines.

- Good risk management must be practiced throughout the organization and be a part of the way it does business.
- Particularly in financial institutions, a separate channel of risk reporting to the Board, via a Chief Risk Office, is warranted.
- Disclosure of foreseeable risks is often poor and can be mechanical and boilerplate in nature. More important is adequate disclosure about the mechanisms of risk management and the risk management culture.
- Remuneration and incentive systems have important implications for risk taking and therefore need to be monitored.

Many Signs Point to the Boards: Can they Cope?

- Board member competence is certainly important but there is no necessary trade-off between independence and competence.
- Boards in many cases appear to remain captured by their own histories and by management so that they may be reactive rather than proactive. Individual members are seldom changed by being voted out of office by shareholders, indicating significant path dependency.
- Separating the CEO from the Chairman position should be regarded as good practice and not as required practice. Disclosure is important. Companies should explain

the reasons for choosing their leadership structure and disclose the Corporate Governance arrangements that they put in place.

- There might be a need to strengthen the legal duties of Board members and to improve enforcement possibilities.
- In the banking sector, there is a good case for strengthening risk reporting lines to the Board and for extending the 'fit and proper person' test to cover the skills and independence of a potential Board member.

Are Shareholders Able to Protect their Interests?

- Shareholders have tended to be reactive rather than proactive and seldom challenge Boards in sufficient number to make a difference.
- The share of institutional investors continues to increase but their voting behaviour suggests reluctance on the part of many to play an active role.
- It should be considered as good practice for institutional investors acting in a fiduciary capacity to disclose their voting records in order to make more transparent any conflicts of interest and how they are being managed.
- Institutional investors (and others) should not be discouraged from acting together in individual shareholders' meetings, provided that they do not intend to obtain control of the company.
- Measures should be taken to remove obstacles and to

encourage the use of flexible voting mechanisms such as electronic voting.

- As the share of institutional shareholders increases, greater attention has turned to proxy advisors and to the potential for conflicts of interest.
- The role of alternative investors (private equity funds and activist hedge funds) should not be hampered as a side effect of regulatory reforms that might be developed to address the specific issues that have created problems.
- Stronger complementarity between private and public enforcement instruments could contribute to creating a more favourable framework for active informed shareholders.

Challenges: Current Oversight Concerns and Regulatory Developments

Current Oversight Concerns

Corporate governance refers to the manner in which the affairs of a corporate body are or should be conducted in order to serve and protect the individual and collective interests of all stakeholders.

Corporate governance became a pressing issue following the 1992 introduction of the Sarbanes-Oxley Act in the US, which was ushered in to restore public confidence in companies and markets after accounting fraud bankrupted high profile companies such as Enron and WorldCom. Most companies strive to have a high level of corporate governance. These days it is not enough for a company to merely be profitable; it also needs to demonstrate good corporate citizenship through environmental awareness, ethical behaviour and sound corporate governance practices. Corporate governance is emerging as a basic component of success in terms of the functioning of the corporate sector in financial markets. In this regard, the Securities and Exchange Commission of Pakistan (SECP) has taken several initiatives for the effectiveness of corporate governance in Pakistan. The addition of independent directors in Pakistani companies is crucial for attaining a better position in the global market by adopting the concept of corporate governance.

Corporate governance in Pakistan is evolving over the years and even now, due to many distortions in the economy, market forces do not reward good governance or punish unethical practices as is expected in an efficient business and governance environment. The huge undocumented economy discourages promotion of transparency and accountability in organizations. The overall management structure is also not conducive to establishing the norms of good governance. Many companies listed on the stock exchanges are complying in form but not fully practicing the Code of Good Governance. Tightly held ownership, lack of professional skills, missing change agents, audit dependability and overall structural weaknesses are bottlenecks in developing corporate governance in organizations and demonstrating its benefits to the business community and the public at large.

The following are the current issues in corporate governance in Pakistan:

INEFFECTIVENESS OF INDEPENDENT NON-EXECUTIVE DIRECTORS (INEDS) IN LISTED COMPANIES OF PAKISTAN

Board composition and independence are fundamental issues in corporate governance. In Pakistan, there is a weak concept of INEDs. Board independence is one of the most important elements of good corporate governance. Independent directors broadly fit into the overall structure of corporate governance, and are necessary to ensure an effective, balanced Board. The Revised Code of Corporate Governance specifies criteria for a person to be considered as an independent director.

In Pakistan, the concept of INEDs is now gaining momentum and companies have started appointing them, but their effectiveness is questionable. The following are some reasons for INEDs being ineffective in Pakistan's listed companies.

Companies Owned by Families or Closed Groups

Companies are mostly owned by families or closed groups and they usually try to stay away from directors whom they are unable to control. Actually, controlling shareholders are keen to run their company in their own way and there is generally resistance to any kind of interference from outside. In Pakistan, a large number of businesses are family-owned and the absolute power is vested with the governing family. The minority shareholders in a real sense do not have any right to effectively participate in decision making and they also do not unite to elect any nominee in the Board for the protection of their rights and interests. Inactiveness, the lack of unity amongst minority shareholders, and the negligible interest in matters regarding the company is the root cause of this discrepancy.

Companies Do Not Pay Remuneration

Another important cause of ineffective INEDs in Pakistan is that companies do not pay adequate compensation or remuneration to them. There is generally a fixed fee for them for attending a meeting. The trend is however changing, and recently companies have started paying enhanced remuneration for non-executive and independent directors.

Insecurity of Interests of Other Stakeholders

Stakeholders other than the shareholders are not as powerful to protect their interests in developing countries like Pakistan. Employees work for long hours at minimum wages, suppliers and customers are not satisfied with the behaviour of the company, and an important problem is the waste and pollution that industries are emitting into the environment. This behaviour of one part of the stakeholders towards the others is the main reason for the ineffectiveness of corporate governance in such companies.

In Pakistan, individuals or entities that are responsible for human rights and environmental protection are not very active. There has recently been an increasing trend of focusing on Corporate Social Responsibility environmental reporting and some companies have started integrated reporting.

UNETHICAL AND DISGRACEFUL BEHAVIOUR

The large size of the informal economy and corrupt practices do have a major bearing on the quality of governance and constrains those who believe that their businesses should be conducted ethically and in a transparent manner. However, there is a need for a targeted struggle against the informal economy and corrupt practices with enhanced accountability, without which the desired results would not be achievable.

CURRENT REGULATORY DEVELOPMENTS

In an endeavour to align our governance regime with the enhanced requirements of the present times and global best practices, the Securities and Exchange Commission of Pakistan (SECP) has approved the Revised Code of Corporate Governance in 2012 and has also approved amendments to certain provisions of the Code of Corporate Governance. The amendments have been made taking into account the lessons learnt from the practical issues and considerations relevant to the listed companies and to ensure that it reflects changing governance concerns, practices, economic circumstances, and best international practices.

The amended provisions relax eligibility requirements for the chief financial officer (CFO) and the head of internal audit (HOIA) for listed companies.

The experience requirements for the CFO have been reduced from five years of handling financial or corporate affairs of a listed company or a bank/financial institution to three years of experience in a public practice (audit/accounting) firm or in managing financial/corporate affairs of a company.

- The experience requirements for HOIA have also been reduced from the earlier restrictive five years of relevant audit experience to three years in audit, finance or compliance function.
- As per an earlier clarification issued by the SECP, experience in a public practice (audit/accounting) firm would also be considered relevant audit experience.

Moreover, the mandatory condition of appointing an independent director as chairman of the audit committee has been made voluntary to facilitate companies in appointing suitably qualified non-executive directors as chairman of the said committee.

These amendments have been approved following a review focused primarily on further refining the practicality of the code for listed companies. The said amendments are expected to improve compliance with the code and encourage new entrants to the fields of finance, audit and related functions, thereby expanding the existing talent pool of professionals in the country.

CONCLUSIONS

The focus on financial stewardship—which is primarily the role of the Board of the company—and accountability are the key factors to improve the business environment and quality of governance. Pakistan is categorized amongst the lowest level of countries in respect of 'Ease of doing business', social and human resource indicators, and unethical corrupt practices.

The Code of Corporate Governance in Pakistan has over the last 12 years contributed to a great extent to improve the quality of governance, disclosures and accountability, but there is still a long way to go to achieve an optimum level.

The government in general and regulators, including institutions responsible for self-regulation, have to follow a targeted strategy to struggle against the informal economy and corrupt practices with a clearly defined action plan and key performance indicators to fully exploit the potential of the country, its resources, and people. The initial target should be to reduce the size of the informal economy by at least 50 per cent in the next 3–5 years.

Accountability is vital for all business activities but more so for the corporate sector and all public interest entities by strengthening institutions and enabling them to independently play their role.

The oversight of the auditing profession has been a subject of debate between regulators and professional bodies such as the ICAP, including the quality control mechanism of the ICAP. There have been proposals to have an independent Oversight Board to monitor the quality and performance of auditors to ensure that the continuing gap between the profession and the perception of the users of financial statements is narrowed and the credibility of the financial statements is further enhanced. Institutions like credit rating agencies, the Competition Commission of Pakistan, Federal Board of Revenue and SECP have to be transformed into more transparent and professionally more effective organizations. Accountability has to be non-discriminatory and fair and institutional frameworks need to be strengthened. There has recently emerged evidence of activism in some of the above institutions, which has to be a continuous process, the test of which would be when everyone would start believing that there is no way to get away with any non-compliance or corrupt practices. Corporate governance is a dynamic process and would require a greater focus over a period of time to ensure that it remains relevant and effective in the challenging and fast changing business environment.

The best practices in other jurisdictions need to be continuously ascertained and focused on. The core aspect of good governance and accountability is ensuring that the entity has a 'governance culture'. The governance of individual companies depends on culture. The Board has the responsibility for shaping the culture within the boardroom and across the organization. This would require consistent vigilance and assessment that the culture practiced is in line with what is espoused. The assurance the Board would require around the culture inter alia would include the following:

- Are performance drivers and values consistent?
- Is the culture followed consistently throughout the business?
- Is the risk management deeply embedded in the organization's culture?
- Ensure stress testing to ascertain how culture can be maintained under pressure and through change.

Chapter 7

Protecting Stakeholders' Rights

Dr Parvez Hassan

INTRODUCTION

Pakistan, like India, inherited at Partition in 1947 the Companies Act, 1913 as a major legislation in the field of corporate regulation. But three developments since the 1970s have reoriented the developments in this sector toward democratisation and better protection of the rights of all stakeholders:

1. Companies (Managing Agency and Election of Directors) Order, 1972 (P.O. 2 of 1972);
2. Companies Ordinance, 1984 (the Companies Ordinance), and
3. Code of Corporate Governance, 2002 (the Code).

P.O. 2 of 1972, one of the boldest reforms introduced by Zulfikar Ali Bhutto post-1970 elections, prohibited the 'colonialist' managing agency system that allowed siphoning off funds and corporate profits to managing agents. Another salutary effect of P.O. 2 of 1972 was the introduction of cumulative voting for the election of directors of Pakistani companies. The Companies Act, 1913 had, for long, enabled a 51 per cent shareholder to appoint all the directors of a company. But the P.O. 2 of 1972 changed this to enable minority shareholders to also elect their own directors.

The Companies Ordinance substituted the Companies Act, 1913 and incorporated the provisions of P.O. 2 of 1972 into the new mainstream law. I had the privilege to assist my good friend, Mr Irtiza Hussain, Chairman, Corporate Law Authority, in the finalization of the 1984 Ordinance.[1] This Companies Ordinance innovated with provisions on minority oppression, investments in associated companies, and conduct of Board meetings. An important commitment to democratising the corporate sector had commenced.

The Code of Corporate Governance, 2002, was an excellent initiative of the Securities and Exchange Commission of Pakistan (SECP) to reinforce and further strengthen the democratisation of the corporate sector. The regulatory roles of the Stock Exchanges in Karachi, Lahore and Islamabad were fully utilized to apply the Code to all the listed companies. The more cumbersome route of amending the Companies Ordinance to include provisions of the Code was avoided in favour of the imaginative recourse to the regulatory powers of the stock exchanges to anchor the Code. The Code was significantly revised in 2012.

This chapter will address corporate governance in Pakistan principally through the prism of the above milestones in respect of the major stakeholders, i.e. the shareholders, directors and creditors of Pakistani companies. Parallel developments through the Securities Exchange Ordinance, 1969 and the Monopolies and Restrictive Trade Practices (Control and

Prevention) Ordinance, 1970 and the establishment of the Securities Exchange Authority of Pakistan (SEAP) and the Monopoly Control Authority (MCA) respectively under these Ordinances facilitated a professional regulation of the corporate sector beyond the institutional framework of the Registrar Companies under the Companies Act, 1913. The MCA developed into the Competition Commission under the new Competition Act, 2010. One would also need to acknowledge the supportive jurisprudence developed by the superior judiciary of Pakistan in protecting the rights of all the stakeholders in the corporate sector.

MAIN ELEMENTS OF GOOD CORPORATE GOVERNANCE IN PAKISTAN

Let us consider the principal elements today in the advancement of the interest of all stakeholders and good governance in the corporate sector of Pakistan.

1. Board of Directors

Under the Companies Ordinance, the Board of Directors is the repository of all corporate powers, except those powers which, by law, are to be undertaken by the shareholders or such powers that have been given to the shareholders under the Articles of Association or by a special resolution of the Company. Section 196 of the Companies Ordinance vests the directors[2] with almost all the powers over the operation and management of the Company until they are removed.[3] Barring the matters that have to be decided by the shareholders, all the rest of the powers lie with the directors. To support this director-shareholder dichotomy, the Lahore High Court has held that the shareholders cannot undertake functions allowed to the Board under law.[4] The popular impression that shareholder action can override the Board has been corrected.

The Board is elected for three year terms on the basis of cumulative voting enabling, for example, a 40 per cent shareholder to elect four directors on a ten member Board (Sections 178 and 180). The Board may appoint a Chief Executive Officer who, if not already a director, shall be deemed to be a director of the company (Sections 199 and 200).

In accordance with Section 196(2), there are certain powers that the directors shall exercise on behalf of the company only by means of a resolution passed at their meeting.[5] This requirement of a Board meeting at which certain decisions are to be taken was a departure from the earlier provisions in the Companies Act, 1913, which enabled a Board to take all its decisions without a Board meeting through circulating resolutions.

There are strict provisions in the Companies Ordinance for disclosure of interest/conflict of interest of directors (Sections 215 and 216) and non-compliance may result in a court holding that the director lacks fiduciary behaviour (Section 217) and the ineligibility of being appointed a director of any company for a period of five years (Section 187 (g)).

The directors of a company have a fiduciary duty towards the company, which includes (a) the exercising of their powers for the purposes for which they were conferred and bona fide for the benefit of the company as a whole; (b) ensuring that they do not put themselves in a position in which their duties to the company and their personal interests may conflict, and (c) the duty to take care of the company.[6]

If the directors have acted in a reasonable manner and made decisions that, in their discretion, are profitable to the company, they are said to have fulfilled their fiduciary duties.

2. Rights of the Majority and Emerging Checks and Balances

The majority of the ownership of a company, i.e. the majority shareholders, are given basic rights under the Companies Ordinance in the stewardship of the company. At 51 per cent ownership, they can elect a majority of the directors (Section 178) and thereby appoint the Chief Executive Officer of the company (Section 199). The majority control of the Board also enables the appointment of other principal officers such as the Chief Financial Officer and Secretary of the company as well as ongoing control of the management of the business and affairs of the company (Section 196). Through a 51 per cent shareholding, at the annual general meeting they can approve annual accounts, approve dividends, and appoint statutory auditors (Sections 158 and 160). With 75 per cent shareholding, at annual general meetings they can pass special resolutions by not less than a three-fourth majority (Section 2(36)), including to amend the Memorandum and Articles of

Association (Sections 21 and 28) and to approve investments in associated undertakings (Section 208).

But the Companies Ordinance, in parallel, also provides a system of checks and balances whereunder the minority shareholders play an important role in corporate governance. Thus, a 25 per cent plus minority shareholding can block any special resolution. Similarly, although a Chief Executive Officer can be appointed by a majority of the Board of Directors, unless otherwise provided in the Articles of Association, his removal is possible only by a resolution passed by not less than three-fourths of the total number of directors or by a special resolution of the company (Section 202), thus ensuring the participation of minority shareholders.

3. Minority Protection

Section 108 of the Companies Ordinance provides that if 10 per cent or more of the class of shareholders are aggrieved by any variation of their rights, they may, within 30 days of the date of the resolution varying their rights, apply to the High Court for an order cancelling the resolution. The Court is thus entrusted with the task of ensuring that these shareholders are not the victims of any unfair prejudice.

Section 289 of the Companies Ordinance provides for minority shareholder protection in the event of transfer of shares between companies. It binds the transferring company to acquire the shares of dissenting shareholders on the same terms as the ones on which shares of the approving shareholders are being acquired. It also states that a transfer of shares between companies requires the approval of at least nine-tenth of the holders of the company's shares in terms of value.

Section 86 of the Companies Ordinance provides that where directors decide to increase the capital of the company by the issuance of further shares, such shares are to be issued to each existing member strictly in proportion to his present shareholding, irrespective of the class of shares held.[7]

A 10 per cent minority shareholding is entitled to the appointment of inspectors to investigate the affairs of a company (Section 263). This has proved to be an important right to enforce accountability of the management of the company.

Minority oppression is directly dealt with and included in Sections 290 to 295 of the Companies Ordinance. Building on Section 153-C of the Companies Act, 1913, added in 1979, Section 290 of the Companies Ordinance provides a remedy to the minority shareholders holding not less than 20 per cent of the issued capital of a company (the threshold in Section 153-C was 10 per cent) to file a petition in the High Court if, inter alia, the affairs of the company are being conducted in an unlawful manner or in a manner oppressive to the minority shareholders. Section 290 gives wide and vast powers to the High Courts to take corrective measures by passing appropriate orders if it is shown that the affairs of the company are being conducted, or are likely to be conducted, in an unlawful or fraudulent manner or in a manner prejudicial to public interest or in a manner oppressive to the members.

The jurisprudence in this area has developed to well protect minority shareholders. It has been held that the affairs of the company can be conducted oppressively[8] by the directors doing nothing to defend its interest when they ought to do something, just as they can conduct its affairs oppressively by doing something injurious to its interests when they ought not to. The majority depriving minority shareholders of their lawful rights and share in the company business is a prima facie case of oppression.[9] It has further been held that a shareholder complaining of 'oppression' must show that he has been constrained to submit to conduct which lacks in probity, conduct that is unfair to him and which causes prejudice to him in the exercise of his legal and proprietary rights as a shareholder.[10]

Further, with respect to schemes of merger and amalgamation, the superior courts of Pakistan have disapproved schemes which, as proposed, work seriously to the disadvantage of the shareholders and on the face of the record are unconscionable and grossly unfair to the minority shareholders of the company.[11]

The courts have, in respect of the provisions regarding minority oppression, more often gone into the requisites for actions under the Companies Ordinance rather than dealing with the question of what constitutes oppression. Some principles established by them in this regard are:

1. The majority depriving minority shareholders of their lawful rights and share in the company business is a prima facie case of oppression. The existence of a state of deadlock between parties and the complete lack of confidence between the minority shareholders and the

majority shareholders are just and equitable grounds for winding up of a company.[12]

2. An attempt to oust the minority shareholders through the induction of a third party constitutes an act of oppression.[13]
3. A prima facie case has to be brought to the court, and in such a case there is nothing that prevents the courts from lifting the veil of incorporation to determine the nature of the relationship between the shareholders.[14]
4. Minority oppression under Section 290 occurs when the conduct of the majority towards the minority shareholders is:

   (a) burdensome, harsh and wrongful; (b) lacking in probity or unfair and prejudicial, and (c) consecutive and has a continuous effect. Events shall have to be considered not in isolation but as part of a consecutive story.[15]

5. The remedy provided to the oppressed under Section 290 is preventive in nature.[16]
6. The petitioner has to be a current or present member of the company holding not less than 20 per cent of the issued share capital of the company.[17]

Minority shareholders further have the right, under Section 305 (f) (iii) of the Companies Ordinance, to get the company wound up by a court if they are of the opinion that the company has conducted business in a manner that is oppressive to them.[18]

4. Rights of Creditors

The Companies Ordinance also took a quantum jump in addressing and strengthening the rights of creditors in the management of companies. The Companies Act, 1913 had, generally, limited the rights of creditors to be consulted at the time of the winding up of a company (Section 174) or during an amalgamation/reconstruction/compromise of companies (Section 153). These continued in Sections 320 and 284 of the Companies Ordinance.

But the Companies Ordinance broke new ground. It enables companies to have 'directors nominated by the company's creditors or other special interests by virtue of contractual arrangements' (Sections 182 and 183). Another important right pioneered for certain creditors is provided in Section 87:

> **87. Issue of Shares in Lieu of Outstanding Balance of any Loans, etc.**
>
> Notwithstanding anything contained in section 86 or the memorandum and articles, a company may issue ordinary shares or grant option to convert into ordinary shares the outstanding balance of any loans, advances or credit, as defined in the Banking Companies Ordinance, 1962 (LVII of 1962), or other non-interest bearing securities and obligations outstanding or having a term of not less than three years in the manner provided in any contract with any scheduled bank or a financial institution to the extent of 20 per cent of such balance ...

Importantly, Section 290 of the Companies Ordinance enables creditors having an interest equivalent to 20 per cent of the paid up capital of the company to invoke the relief mechanisms against the borrower company provided in Section 290. It is noted that this was a new right of the creditors as it was not included in the earlier Section 153-C of the Companies Act, 1913, as added in 1979. The marked difference between the earlier Section 153-C of the Companies Act, 1913, and Section 290 of the Companies Ordinance is that the interest of the creditor is to be taken into account while considering an application under the latter.[19]

But by far the most-used right by creditors is to invoke the winding up of a company on the ground that it is unable to pay its debts (Sections 305(e) and 306).

5. Investments in Associated Undertakings

Section 208 of the Companies Ordinance regulates investment in associated undertakings and associated companies, irrespective of the amount of investment. The courts in Pakistan have adopted a rather clear and strict approach in interpreting this Section.

Section 2 (2) of the Companies Ordinance defines 'associated companies' and 'associated undertakings' as any two or more companies or undertakings, or a company and an undertaking, interconnected with each other in certain ways such as through an inter-locking common management and common control or through an inter-locking common holding of 20 per cent of the voting power of the companies or undertakings.

Under Section 208, investments in associated companies shall not be made by any company in any of its associated companies or associated undertakings except under the prior authority of a special resolution passed after discussing the potential investment with the shareholders of the company.

This special resolution includes the nature, period and amount of investment and terms and conditions attached thereto and it is also provided by the Companies Ordinance, as per Section 208 (2), that no change in the nature of an investment or the terms and conditions attached thereto shall be made except under the authority of a special resolution. While the scope of what constitutes an investment in an associated company is rather wide, such as loans, equity, and advances as per the proviso, the Companies Ordinance strictly provides that the return on investment in the form of a loan shall not be less than the borrowing cost of the investing company.

Furthermore, it is provided by Section 208 (2) that every director of a company who is 'knowingly and wilfully in default' shall be liable to a fine that may extend to one million rupees and in addition, the directors shall jointly and severally reimburse to the company any loss sustained by the company in consequence of an investment that was made without complying with the requirements of this Section.[20]

The essential elements in respect of this Section, developed mostly in case law decided by the SECP, are as follows:

1. A special resolution must be passed if any investment

in an associated company or associated undertaking is to take effect. A special resolution, defined in Section 2(36) of the Companies Ordinance, denotes a resolution which has been passed by at least three-fourths of members entitled to vote at a general meeting. Unless a special resolution is passed and filed, any investment in an associated company will be in violation of the provisions of the Companies Ordinance.[21] The Companies Ordinance does not permit any subsequent ratification of investments made by companies in their associated concerns.[22] Merely emphasizing that the company has gained numerous advantages from an investment in an associated company would not relieve the company from obtaining the mandatory shareholders' resolution in terms of Section 208 of the Companies Ordinance.[23]

2. The special resolution must be passed following an attachment of a notice, which includes in it the nature, period and amount of the investment. If the resolution has failed to include the above mentioned elements before passing the resolution, then such a resolution will be held to be not in accordance with the provisions of the Companies Ordinance.[24] Where the directors of the company have tried to conceal the correct information, or not provided timely information to the shareholders, it was held that the directors of that company deserved no sympathy on that account.[25]
3. The directors of the company owe fiduciary duties to the company they serve and to its shareholders; they must discharge their statutory obligations

with reasonable care and in good faith, fairness and honesty.[26] Section 208 (3) provides that each director who is 'knowingly and wilfully in default' in complying with the requirements set out above under Section 208 will be liable. Although the provision does not define the terms 'knowingly and wilfully in default', case law points out that when ascertaining whether there was a wilful default, three elements must be present: (a) the doer or abstainer of the act or omission must be a free agent; (b) he must be conscious of what he is doing or not doing and the probable result that might arise from his act, and (c) this default may range from a state of mind all the way from supine indifference to conscious violation as a result of deliberation.[27]

6. Insider Trading

Section 15A of the Securities and Exchange Commission of Pakistan Ordinance, 1969 (the SECP Ordinance) provides that no person shall indulge in 'insider trading'. 'Insider trading' has been defined in Section 15A(2) as including 'an insider person transacting any deal, directly or indirectly, using inside information involving listed securities to which the inside information pertains, or using others to transact such deals.' 'Inside information' is information that has not been made public, relating, directly or indirectly, to listed securities or one or more issuers and which, if it were made public, would be likely to have an effect on the prices of those listed securities or on the price of related securities (Section 15B).

Section 15C provides that insiders include sponsors, executive officers and directors of an issuer, which is a person who has issued any security.

The liability of insider trading, provided in Section 15E, includes the liability to pay a fine, 'which may extend to ten million rupees or three times the amount of gain made or loss avoided by such person, or loss suffered by another person, whichever amount is higher.'

The Companies Ordinance creates a category of shareholders popularly referred to as 'insiders' of a company and regulates the trading of shares of the company by such insiders. 'Insiders' include directors, chief executive, chief accountant, secretary or auditor of a listed company and principal shareholders of the company beneficially owning, directly or indirectly, more than 10 per cent of the shares of the company. Section 224 of the Companies Ordinance provides that if any 'insider' makes any gain by the purchase and sale, or the sale and purchase, of any such security, within a period of less than six months, such director, chief executive, chief accountant, secretary or auditor or person who is a beneficial owner shall make a report and tender the amount of such gain to the company and simultaneously send an intimation to this effect to the registrar and the SECP.

To 'monitor' this, the Companies Ordinance requires a periodic report of the beneficial ownership of such insiders as well as any changes in their ownership (Section 222). Any default in reporting the change in beneficial ownership of a company to the SECP attracts a penalty, which may extend to Rs 30,000, or a fine, which may extend to Rs 1,000 every day that the contravention continues (Section 224(4)).

The intention behind the insider trading provisions of Section 224 is to put a check on the directors and other insiders from taking undue advantage of inside information of the company's securities to their benefit. The case law interpreting Section 224 signifies that the purpose of Section 224 is to discourage frauds and collusive transactions meant to usurp the gain through the forbidden activity.[28] It has further been pointed out that the intention of the legislature and objective in respect of Section 224 is to put a check on the directors who in their fiduciary functions are likely to obtain inside information of the company's securities, take undue advantage of such inside information and make a purchase/sale of the shares and as a result thereof make a personal gain.[29]

Recently, the SECP has proposed that insider trading be a criminal offence under the draft Securities Act, 2015,[30] wherein the penalty for insider trading will be imprisonment of three years or a penalty of Rs 200 million or three times the gain. The SECP, under the draft Act, would have the emergency powers to suspend stock market operations in order to inspect proceedings.

7. Winding up of Private Limited Companies

It has developed as an important part of our jurisprudence that a private limited company can be wound up and treated as a partnership firm to the extent as would justify the dissolution of a partnership firm under Section 44 of the Partnership Act, 1932. And the grounds that are available to a partner for having a partnership firm dissolved are also available to a shareholder for the winding-up of a private limited company under the just and equitable clause. The leading authority in this regard is Ladli Prasad Jaiswal vs. The Karnal Distillery Co. Ltd,[31] wherein the Supreme Court held that in the case of a private limited company, the tendency of the courts has uniformly been to treat it more or less as a partnership and to apply the same principles in the winding-up of a private limited company as would entitle a partner to have a partnership firm dissolved. Commonly, the exclusion of the partner from the management of a firm, the existence of a state of deadlock between the partners or a justifiable lack of confidence in the management have been regarded as just and proper grounds for dissolving a private limited company.

In Nagina Films Ltd vs. Usman Hussain,[32] the Karachi High Court, after examination of a number of cases on the subject, enunciated inter alia, the following principles: (a) that the principles of dissolution of partnership may be applied if the apparent structure of the company is not the real structure and on piercing the veil it is found that in reality it is a partnership; (b) generally the exclusion of a partner from the management of the firm; (c) existing of a state of deadlock between the partners; or (d) justifiable lack of confidence in the management have been regarded as just and proper grounds for dissolving a private limited company.

Minority shareholders in private limited companies thus have important safeguards against oppression by the majority by enabling the winding up of the company in almost the same manner as they would dissolve a partnership.

8. Prohibiting Managing Agencies

The introduction of P.O. 2 of 1972 brought in the bold and healthy change of abolishing the 'parasitical institution of managing agencies in Pakistan, which were a legacy of the colonial era'.[33] Although a monumental stride was taken to protect the minority shareholder, this legislation, mostly because of its timing, was received as being anti-business.[34]

The managing agency system was born in India in the nineteenth century. Under this system, the management of a company is given by its directors to a managing agent, a separate corporate entity, which then has a 'relatively free hand in running things'.[35] This system permitted opportunities for funnelling profits and placing them where the shareholders of the actual operating company had no control over them. Under the P.O. 2 of 1972, Dr Mubashir Hasan, the Finance Minister, announced the abolition of the managing agency system, terminating the agents' agreements and contracts without compensation. Control of companies previously handled by the managing agencies was transferred to the directors of the companies. In an article published by *Pakistan Times,* Dr Hasan pointed out that:

'Managing agencies were one of the worst institutions of loot and plunder through which the cream of profits was skimmed by a handful of people who were able to control capital ... They had a complete stranglehold over the industry.'[36]

The bar on appointment of managing agencies is now included in Section 206 of the Companies Ordinance with enabling exceptions.

9. Responsive and Protective Judiciary

Beyond the statutory and regulatory framework for protecting the rights of all the stakeholders in corporate management, the superior judiciary of Pakistan has provided effective safeguards to all. Time and again, the courts have adopted a rule of law-based approach in interpreting the rights of the stakeholders in the corporate sector. Thus, when notices for a meeting of the Board were not sent to all the directors, the meeting and any resolution passed at such meeting were held not to be valid.[37] Similarly, when the shareholders were entitled to receive certain statutory information with respect to decisions to be taken at a shareholder meeting, the meeting could not transact the business to a decision without receiving such information. It was mandatory for such information to be provided without which any resolution would stand vitiated.[38]

The powers of the High Courts in respect of minority protection remain vast and undefined.[39] The jurisprudence in respect of Section 290 of the Companies Ordinance reflects that although the judiciary will attempt to remedy the oppression and mismanagement on the part of the controlling shareholders/directors, it will not interfere with past or concluded transactions between the company and third parties.[40] All material factors are considered in taking a decision[41] and an isolated event would usually not warrant interference by the judiciary.[42] Moreover, the judiciary remains cautious in respect of the remedy provided and is quick to ensure that the remedies are proportionate to the mismanagement. The object, it appears, is not to settle disputes between the parties or to curb the creativity of the management,[43] but rather that the affairs of a company be conducted in a lawful manner[44] and in the interest of justice.

Normally, courts will not intervene in matters regarding the internal (and indoor) management of a company; hence where the directors are acting within the powers conferred on them by the Articles of Association, the courts will rarely interfere.[45] For example, removal of a director does not amount to oppression or exclusion of minority shareholders.[46]

Furthermore, although the option for winding up is available to the courts, the courts will seldom allow such an extreme relief where, instead, a remedy under Section 290 is available.[47]

10. Other Laws

1. Stock Exchanges

The Karachi, Lahore and Islamabad Stock Exchanges also watch the interests of the public and minority shareholders. The Listing Regulations incorporate the Code and require that all listed companies go beyond the regime of the Companies Ordinance with respect to the protection extended to minority shareholders and (a) encourage representation of non-executive directors representing minority interests; (b) encourage minority representation by proxy solicitation; and (c) in the event of any divestiture of shares, offer, in writing, to the minority shareholders the same price for the acquisition of their shares.

2. Securities and Exchange Ordinance, 1969.

Reacting to the slogan of the twenty two families,[48] the government in the late 1960s introduced two laws, the Securities and Exchange Ordinance, 1969 and the Monopolies and Restrictive Trade Practices (Control and Prevention) Ordinance, 1970. These laws were borrowed from the US and at least one of them was even drafted by an American law professor. Both those laws, it is submitted, were far ahead of their time and were not applicable to the prevailing economic factors in Pakistan. These may have been entirely appropriate for a country with a sophisticated corporate marketplace but not for Pakistan, which was in the embryonic stage of economic development.[49]

The Securities Ordinance,[50] for example, introduced the provisions of insider trading and six monthly reports. Insider trading, in its application, is an extremely sophisticated concept whereby the directors or principal shareholders of a company cannot make personal gains in the trading of the shares of their company. Similarly, the Securities Ordinance required each company to send unaudited six-monthly accounts.

As if the Registrar of Joint Stock Companies, Controller of Capital Issues and the Stock Exchanges were not adequate, the Securities Ordinance added another regulatory agency to the growing list: the Securities and Exchange Authority of Pakistan, later the Corporate Law Authority under the Companies Ordinance.

In 1997, the Securities and Exchange Commission of Pakistan, vide the SECP Act, 1997, succeeded the Corporate

Law Authority, which was an attached department of the Ministry of Finance, to become the autonomous regulator of the corporate sector of Pakistan. The scope of the authority of the SECP has been extensively widened since its creation. The insurance sector, non-banking financial companies, and pension funds have been added to the purview of the SECP. The SECP also regulates various external service providers that are linked to the corporate sector, like chartered accountants, rating agencies, and corporate secretaries.

3. Monopolies and Restrictive Trade Practices (Control and Prevention) Ordinance, 1970 (the Monopolies Control Ordinance) and the Competition Act, 2010.

The Monopolies Control Ordinance was specifically anti-big business and sought to eliminate cartels and monopolies in Pakistan. Inspired by the US anti-trust experience, the Monopolies Control Ordinance outlawed (a) undue concentration of economic power, (b) unreasonable monopoly power, and (c) unreasonably restrictive trade practices. These concepts were elaborated to prohibit market fixing, price leadership and tying arrangements, all areas of innovation but of little relevance to local conditions at that time. The Monopolies Control Ordinance also included comprehensive registration requirements for situations that may border on any of the above areas. To the ever-growing list of corporate ombudsmen, the Monopolies Ordinance added yet another agency called the Monopoly Control Authority (MCA) of Pakistan.

Since its implementation, it became apparent that the Monopolies Ordinance did not produce any useful results. No meaningful contravention of this Ordinance had been established and there was much speculation as to the utility of keeping this legislation alive. The scope of the Monopolies Control Ordinance was severely constrained by the Economic Reforms Order, 1972, which resulted in a broad nationalization process that affected the major part of the economy.

In October 2007, the Competition Commission of Pakistan (CCP) was established under the Competition Commission Ordinance, 2007 after dissolving the MCA to 'ensure free competition in all spheres of commercial and economic efficiency and to protect consumers from anti-competitive behaviour'. The Competition Commission Ordinance, 2007 was finally passed as the Competition Act, 2010 (CCA). The CCA includes (a) the definitions of 'dominant position' (Section 2(1)(e)); (b) 'relevant market' (Section 2 (1)(k)); (c) the abuse of a dominant position (Section 3). The CCA is supported by the Competition (Merger Control) Regulations, 2007, that prescribe the regulations in respect of the clearance required before a merger or acquisition by the CCP.

11. Future Potential of the Code

The SECP has come up with an ambitious set of

recommendations to regulate the existing structure of the corporate sector in Pakistan. The Code was introduced by the SECP in early 2002 for the stated purpose of establishing a framework of good corporate governance, whereby a listed company can be managed in compliance with international best practices. The Code has been adopted by all the stock exchanges of the country by way of its incorporation in their respective listing regulations. As a result, all listed companies in Pakistan are now required to comply with the provisions of the Code. The introduction of the Code has been followed by amendments to the Companies Ordinance, which are aimed to strengthen corporate governance in Pakistan. The major thrust of the Code is to restructure the Board of Directors in order to make it accountable to all shareholders, to strengthen internal control systems of corporations, to foster better disclosure, and to strengthen internal and external audit requirements of listed companies.

The Code primarily aims to establish a system whereby a company is directed and controlled by its directors in compliance with the best practice so as to safeguard the interests of diversified stakeholders. It proposes to restructure the composition of the Board of Directors in order to introduce broad-based representation by minority shareholders and by executive and non-executive directors. An illustration of how the Code attempts to protect the interests of minority shareholders is provided under Clause 35 (i) of the Code, which provides that the Board of Directors is encouraged to have a balance of executive and non-executive directors, including independent directors and those representing minority interests with the requisite skills, competence, knowledge and experience so that the Board as a group includes core competencies and diversity, including in gender. Furthermore, the test of independence is strengthened by introducing the concept of 'conflict of interest' in the 2012 Code instead of 'being subservient to any apparent form of interference' in the 2002 Code. Listed companies are required to facilitate the minority shareholders to contest the election of directors by proxy solicitation. The inclusion of non-executive directors on the Board discourages the tendency to protect personal interests and motives at the expense of the minority shareholders.

The Code, furthermore, encourages transparency and openness in respect of corporate affairs and the decision-making process and requires directors to discharge their fiduciary responsibilities in the larger interest of all stakeholders in a transparent, informed, diligent and timely manner. The revised Code includes requirements, such as that the Chairman and the Chief Executive Officer be separate persons, and for the regular evaluation of the performance of the Board, which aims to achieve greater balance of power, accountability, and transparency. The salient features of the Code include setting up of audit committees and internal audit functions by all listed companies.

CONCLUSIONS

The legal and regulatory framework for the corporate sector in Pakistan is responsive to our needs to provide an appropriate playing field for an investor, both domestic and foreign. It provides transparency, openness, fairness, and is particularly sensitive to the interests of minority shareholders and creditors. It enables democratic governance on a Board fully represented on the basis of cumulative voting and with checks and balances requiring effective participation of all the stakeholders. The superior judiciary of Pakistan, supported by the SECP, plays an important role in facilitating good corporate governance in the country.

Notes

1. See, e.g., my articles in this effort, Dr Parvez Hassan: (1) Draft on Companies Ordinance, 1980: A Practitioners Viewpoint, 1983 *All Pakistan Legal Decisions, Journal* at 104–10; (2) Corporate Law Sector in Pakistan: Imperatives for Development, 1983 *All Pakistan Legal Decisions Journal* at 45–54; (3) Management Rights and Minority Protection Under the Companies Ordinance, 1984, 1985 *All Pakistan Legal Decisions, Journal* at 19–28; (4) Government Regulation and the Corporate Sector, *Finance Taxation & Company Law,* February 1972, at 41–2; (5) A Corporate Democracy or Corporate Martial Law, in two parts, a comment on the proposed Draft Companies Ordinance 1980, *Business Recorder,* April 15 and 16, 1981; also in *Finance Taxation & Company Law,* April/May 1981, at 101–05, and (6) Management and Minority Protection under Companies Ordinance, 1984, *Business Recorder,* in two parts, January 18 and 19, 1985; also in *Pakistan & Gulf Economist,* January 12–18, 1985.
2. Section 196 of the Companies Ordinance:

   196. Powers of Directors- (l) The business of a Company shall be managed by the Directors, who may pay all expenses

incurred in promoting and registering the Company, and may exercise all such powers of the Company as are not by this Ordinance, or by the articles, or by a special resolution, required to be exercised by the Company in general meeting.

3. See, generally, Muhammad Suleman Kanjiani vs. Dadex Eternit Limited through Chief Executive, 2009 CLD 1687 (Karachi).
4. See, Abdul Malik vs. Janana De Malucho Textile Mills Limited, PLD 1973 Note 116 (Lahore).
5. The reasoning for the provisions of Section 196(2), as deduced from the judgments of the courts, is that the matters listed in Section 196(2) should receive the benefit of the collective judgment and wisdom of the Board at its meeting. In Muhammad Suleman Kanjiani vs. Dadex Eternit Limited, supra note 3, the Board of Directors had given ex-post facto sanction for capital expenditure already incurred by the Chief Executive Officer of the Company. The Karachi High Court, in this regard, held that such subsequent sanction by the Board of Directors:

   > … not only appears to be against the intent of law but also amounts to 'One Man Rule' depriving the Company from the expertise of the Directors on Board … and deprives a Director from his statutory right to contribute by participating in a meaningful meeting resolving to undertake such expenditures.

   Gower's *Principles of Modern Company Law,* (1997), 6th ed., states that:

   > Where powers are conferred on the directors under articles such as those considered above …, they are conferred upon the directors collectively as a board. Prima facie, therefore, they can be exercised only at a board meeting of which due notice has been given and at which quorum is present ….

> The board will, of course, be able to appoint executive agents or servants of the company but must not delegate the exercise of its discretion. (195 and 196).

A. Ramaiya's *Guide to the Companies Act,* (1998), 14th ed., while discussing Section 292 of the Indian Companies Act, 1956, now repealed by its successor legislation Companies Act, 2013, the analogous provision to Section 196 (2) of the Pakistan Companies Ordinance, states that:

> Where the Board is given any special powers under the articles which the Board otherwise would not have under the Act, they cannot delegate such powers to any one director or a committee of directors or to any other person or body, but must exercise the powers themselves as the Board. Nor can they delegate any powers, the exercise of which requires judgment and discretion on their part (2188).

Johari's *Commentaries on Companies Act,* (2006), Vol. 2, also discussing Section 292 of the Indian Companies Act, 1956, states that:

> The expression 'only by means of resolutions passed at meetings of the Board' is to exclude 'resolutions passed by circulation' as permitted in section 289. The powers specified in clauses (a) to (c) of sub-sec. (1) cannot be exercised by 'resolutions passed by circulation'. They can be exercised 'only by means of resolutions passed at meetings of the Board'. The purpose is to ensure proper discussion at the meeting of Board of Directors.
>
> The Directors can express their views for or against the proposal before voting on it. Thus, all Directors are able to share their experience and wisdom.
>
> The purpose of specifying certain subjects relating to which resolution has to be passed only at meetings is to ensure, as

> far as law can do, that the Directors actively participate in considering the subject ... (1922).

6. There is abundant case law in Pakistan that lays down the abovementioned principles. It was held in the case of J.K Spinning Mills Limited, 2011 CLD 614 (SECP) that:

> Directors of the Company owed fiduciary duties to the Company they served and its shareholders; they must discharge their statutory obligations in good faith with fairness and honestly, by that they breached their said fiduciary duty by providing unnecessary benefits to its associated undertaking where they were major shareholders and thereby acting against the interest of its shareholders.

   See, also, Shaheen Insurance Company, 2013 CLD 2207 (SECP), Credit Insurance Company Limited, 2013 CLD 2274 (SECP), and Takaful Pakistan Limited, 2014 CLD 615 (SECP).
7. See, generally, Naseer A. Sheikh vs. Commissioner of Income Tax, PLD 1992 Supreme Court 276, Progressive Insurance Company Ltd, 2009 CLD 1593 (SECP).
8. 'Oppression' is defined in the *Black's Law Dictionary,* 7th ed., as:

> 1. The act or an instance of unjustly exercising authority or power .... Unfair treatment of minority shareholders by the directors or those in control of the corporation (1121).

   And in Halsbury's *Laws of England,* 4th ed., Vol.7, para 1011, as:

> Conduct amounting to oppression. In this context, 'oppressive' means burdensome, harsh and wrongful. It does not include conduct which is merely inefficient or careless. Nor does it include an isolated incident; there must be a continuing course of oppressive conduct, which must be continuing at the date of the hearing of the petition. Further, the conduct must be such as to be oppressive to the

> petitioner in his capacity as a member; whatever remedies he may have in respect of exclusion from the company's business by being dismissed as an employee or a director, he will have none under the provisions relating to oppression. On the other hand, these provisions are not confined merely to conduct designed to secure pecuniary advantage to the oppressors; they cover the case of wrongful usurpation of authority, even though the affairs of the company prosper in consequence.

In the Companies Ordinance, however, oppression is undefined and it is left to the courts, keeping in view the relevant facts of the case, to determine the definition of 'oppression' (see, generally, Shahamatullah Qureshi vs. Hi-Tech Construction (Pvt.) Ltd, 2004 CLD 640 (Karachi).

9. See, generally, Shahbazuddin Chaudhry vs. Messrs. Services Industries Textiles Limited, PLD 1988 Lahore 1 and Mst. Qamar Loan vs. Kashmiran (Pvt.) Ltd, PLD 1997 Karachi 376.
10. See, generally, Chaudhry Muhammad Hussain vs. Khiali Paper and Board Mills (Private) Limited, 2005 CLD 636 (Lahore).
11. See, generally, Re: Pfizer Laboratories Limited and another, 2003 CLD 1209 (Karachi) and In re: Kohinoor Raiwind Mills Limited and others, 2002 CLD 1747 (Lahore—DB).
12. Qamar Loan vs. Kashmiran (Private) Limited, supra note 9, Razzak Usman vs. Golden Plastics, 1998 CLC 1109 (Karachi), and Khursheed Ismail vs. Unichem Corporation (Pvt.) Ltd, 1996 CLC 1863 (Karachi).
13. Pakistan State Oil Company Limited vs. Pakistan Oil Pipelines Limited, PLD 1993 Karachi 322.
14. Mahenau Agha vs. United Liner Agencies of Pakistan Limited, PLD 1990 Karachi 198.

15. See, generally, Shahbazuddin Chaudhry vs. Messrs. Services Industries Textiles Limited, supra note 9, Needle Industries of India Limited vs. Needle Industries Newey (India) Holdings Limited, AIR 1981 Supreme Court 1298, V.M. Rao vs. Rajeswari Ramakrishan, 1987 Company Cases [Vol.61] 20 (Madras), Devaraj Dhanram vs. Firebricks and Potteries (Private) Limited, 1994 Company Cases [Vol.79] 722, and Re Jermyn Street Turkish Baths Limited, 1971 3All ER 184.
16. Associated Biscuits International Limited vs. English Biscuits Manufacturers (Pvt.) Ltd, 2003 CLD 815 (Karachi).
17. Hassan Al-Adawi vs. Hama International Pvt. Ltd, 2009 CLD 1043 (Karachi), and Shaukat Ali vs. Amin Fabrics Limited, 2008 CLD 837 (Karachi).
18. See, generally, Hassan Al-Adawi vs. Hama International (Private) Limited, supra note 17, and Progressive Insurance Company vs. Securities and Exchange Commission of Pakistan, 2009 CLD 1602 (SECP). The courts will however, allow this option hesitantly: Habib Bank Ltd vs. Golden Plastic (Pvt.) Ltd, 1991 MLD 124 (Karachi).
19. Nagina Films Limited vs. Usman Hussain, 1987 CLC 2263 (Karachi).
20. See, generally, Additional Registrar of Companies SECP vs. Speedways Founmetall Limited 2009 CLD 1106 (Karachi).
21. See, generally, Bestway Cement Limited 2009 CLD 56 (SECP) and East West Insurance Company Limited, 2009 CLD 1191 (SECP).
22. See, generally, Gharibwal Cement 2003 CLD 131 (SECP), Monnoo Industries Limited vs. Executive Director, SECP, 2012 CLD 691 (SECP), and Bestway Cement Limited, 2007 CLD 370 (SECP).
23. See, generally, Al Abid Silk Mills Limited 2009 CLD 65 (SECP), and In the matter of Honda Atlas Cars Limited, 2007 CLD 557 (SECP).
24. See, generally, Bosicor Pakistan Limited 2008 CLD 436 (SECP).

25. See, generally, In the matter of Shakarganj Mills Limited, 2007 CLD 1291 (SECP).
26. See, generally, JDW Sugar Mills Limited, 2008 CLD 809 (SECP).
27. In Pakistan Paper Corporation Limited vs. Secretary Federal Minister of Finance, 1984 CLC 2456 (Karachi) and Pak-American Fertilizers Limited vs. Industrial Court Lahore, PLD 1966 Lahore 822, the definition of 'wilful' as defined in the *Black Law Dictionary* was reproduced as 'an act done with stubborn purpose, but not with malice, as done intentionally, knowingly and purposely as distinct from an act done carelessly, thoughtlessly, heedlessly or inadvertently'. In Crescent Steel and Allied Product Limited, 2007 CLD 1060 (SECP), it was held that where the directors had failed to exercise reasonable care to see that mandatory provisions of law were being violated and had not respected the mandate of the shareholders, they had, in circumstances breached their fiduciary duties which they owed to the company and its shareholders by making unauthorized transactions out of the funds of the company, which amounts to 'wilful default'. Acts of making unauthorized investments having been done prior to obtaining of legal opinion, was construed as wilful, In the matter of Honda Atlas Cars Limited, supra note 23.
28. See, generally, First Capital Securities Corporation Limited vs. Commissioner (Securities Market), SECP, Islamabad, 2006 CLD 371 (SECP); First Capital Securities Corporation Limited vs. Commissioner (Securities Market Division) SECP, 2005 CLD 1255 (Lahore); SECP vs. First Capital Securities Corporation Limited, 2011 CLD 907 (Supreme Court).
29. See Tariq Baig, Managing Director, Tariq Glass Industries Limited vs. Executive Director (SM), Securities and Exchange Commission of Pakistan, Islamabad, 2002 CLD 1346 (SECP).

30. Sohail Sarfraz, Draft Securities Act: Insider Trading declared Criminal Offence, *Business Recorder,* March 6, 2015.
31. PLD 1965 Supreme Court 221.
32. Nagina Films Ltd vs. Usman Hussain, supra note 19. See also Associated Biscuits International Limited vs. English Biscuits Manufacturers (Private) Limited, supra note 17; Iqbal Alam vs. Plasticrafters (Private) Limited, 1991 CLC 589 (Karachi); and Kruddson Limited, Karachi, PLD 1972 Karachi 376.
33. See, Dr Parvez Hassan, Corporate Law Sector in Pakistan: Imperatives for Development, supra note 1, at 50.
34. Id.
35. See, W.E. Gustafson, *Economic Reforms under the Bhutto Regime,* University of California, Davis, U.S.A.
36. *Pakistan Times,* January 17, 1972.
37. Iftikhar Hussain Khan of Mamdot vs. Ghulam Nabi Corporation Limited, PLD 1971 Supreme Court 550.
38. M. Shahid Saigol vs. Kohinoor Mills Limited, PLD 1995 Lahore 264. See, also, East West Insurance Company, 2009 CLD 1197 (SECP), Babri Cotton Mills Limited vs. State, 2009 CLD 541 (SECP), Kohinoor Raiwind Mills Limited vs. Kohinoor Gujar Khan Mills, 2002 CLD 1214 (Lahore), Bestway Cement Limited, 2009 CLD 56 (SECP), and Zahur Cotton Mills Limited, 2007 CLD 1271 (SECP).
39. In January 2013, the SECP, vide a press release, notified that it shall set up a task force for better protection of minority shareholders. The object of such task force was, inter alia, to consider establishing a permanent platform for dialogue and cooperation on minority issues, grievance handling and dispute resolution, redressal for violation of rights, identify weaknesses in current protection mechanisms. See, generally, Shaheen Foundation vs. Capital F.M. Pvt. Ltd, 2002 CLD 188 (Karachi).

40. See, Associated Biscuits International Ltd vs. English Biscuits Manufacturers (Private) Limited, supra note 16.
41. Mst. Qamar Loan vs. Kashmirian Pvt. Ltd, supra note 9.
42. Associated Biscuits International Ltd vs. English Biscuits Manufacturers (Private) Limited, supra, note 16.
43. See, generally, Muhammad Hussain vs. Khiali Paper and Board Mills (Pvt.) Ltd, supra note 10.
44. See, generally, (Muhammad Fikree vs. Fikree Development Corporation Ltd), 1992 MLD 668 (Karachi).
45. See, Shahamatullah Qureshi vs. Hi-Tech Construction (Pvt.) Ltd, supra note 8.
46. Shahbazuddin Chaudhry vs. Messrs. Services Industries Textiles Ltd, supra note 9.
47. See, generally, Habib Bank Ltd vs. Golden Plastic (Pvt.) Ltd, 1991 MLD 124 (Karachi), and WAPDA vs. Kot Addu Power Company Ltd, PLD 2000 Lahore 461.
48. The phrase 'twenty two families' became a metaphor for Pakistan's economic distribution. It was initially used by Dr Mahboob-ul-Haque, the chief economist of Pakistan's Planning Commission in 1968 to describe the pattern of economic distribution in the country, namely that 22 families owned 66 per cent of industrial, 70 per cent of insurance, and 80 per cent of banking assets. M. A. Qadeer, *Pakistan: Social and Cultural Transformations in a Muslim Nation,* (2006). See also, generally, Dr Parvez Hassan, The 22 Families and After, *Outlook,* April 28, 1973.
49. See, generally, Dr Parvez Hassan, Corporate Law Sector in Pakistan: Imperatives for Development, supra note 1.
50. For a discussion of its salient provisions, see Dr Parvez Hassan, Securities and Exchange Ordinance, 1969, 3 *Finance Taxation & Company Law,* 97–100 (1971).

PART III

Practical Application: Implementing in Letter and Spirit

Chapter 8

Raising the Bar for Director Education

Fuad Azim Hashimi

'I have been a director for so many years. What are you going to teach me?'

Such a response was not uncommon when Pakistan Institute of Corporate Governance (PICG) first engaged in director education. PICG came into being as a cooperative initiative undertaken by the Securities and Exchange Commission of Pakistan (SECP) and International Finance Corporation (IFC) in 2004. IFC through its Corporate Governance Project (PCGP) was charged with building capacity to enable PICG to achieve laid-down objectives, one of which was director education. As good governance practices in the corporate sector emulate the 'tone at the top', the responsibility would rest solely with the Board of Directors.

During the initial years, PICG went through a learning phase. Two important events took place. Firstly, the World Bank conducted and produced a Report on the Observance of Standards and Codes (ROSC) in 2005 related to governance practices in Pakistan, which showed some gaps and perhaps justified the implementation of PCGP. And, a few years later, in 2007, IFC sponsored a Survey of Corporate Governance

Practices in Pakistan. The survey showed over 90 per cent compliance with good governance practices as required by the Code of Corporate Governance 2002 but was critical of such compliance being more of a 'box-ticking' exercise. As a consequence, while PICG was pursuing its primary objective of increasing awareness of good governance practices in the corporate sector, it additionally began to focus on director education. After all, good governance is not so much about regulation but more about bringing about a change in behaviour, a change in one's mind and heart!

IFC had already rolled out a director education programme in Egypt based on the Board Development Series (BDS) that had been researched and put together by the Global Corporate Governance Forum (GCGF). However it needed adaptation to Pakistan's Company Law. So PICG, with this adaptation and with IFC's support, put out the first director education programme in February 2007. At the time, BDS was designed as an eight day, four part, workshop-based programme with little or no case studies. To assist PICG in the delivery, IFC undertook to provide its international faculty for the first time round that each part was held. On its part PICG identified individuals experienced in Board matters to sit in as observers so that they could take over and facilitate the next time such sessions were held. There was additionally a written comprehensive examination that had to be taken after attending all the four parts and comprising 192 questions! This was a tall order indeed for some who were still heard to say, 'I have been a director for so many years. What are you going to teach me?'

To attract such individuals into director training was not

easy. A good amount of networking was required and as a sweetener, it made sense to seek international accreditation for this programme. IFC arranged this with Institutional Shareholders Services (ISS) in the US, who would effectively consider for better credit-worthiness those corporations who had Board members who had undergone director education. During the first period of three years that PICG ran this programme, we had 16 intakes (also known as cohorts in academia) engaging 301 participants of which only 169 attained certification – certification being awarded to those who stayed the course and satisfactorily cleared the comprehensive examination. ISS became part of the Risk Metrics Group, USA and Risk Metrics decided that as compliance with good governance practices had become an international norm, they would discontinue accrediting director education programmes.

In the meanwhile, GCGF had received substantial feedback since rolling out BDS and had engaged a group of experienced governance professionals to develop a new programme, Corporate Governance Leadership Skills (CGLS), which was being rolled out as a toolkit. While PICG had taken the lead in IFC's Middle East North Africa region (MENA) in holding BDS successfully and in making the comprehensive examination an online testing process held after each part, it had found through participant evaluation of the programme that it was too lengthy and at times too basic. The new CGLS was a four-and-a-half day, five-part programme and provided a much desired solution, especially as it was built around a case study of a hypothetical company and participants would be engaged in different exercises related to that case study throughout the programme. The countrywise rollout by IFC was however subject to a prerequisite of the trainers being trained.

With IFC's support, PICG embarked on a regular training of trainers so that a body of visiting faculty would become available when CGLS was rolled out. An important element of the success of PICG's director education programme is not the course content alone but also the skill sets its visiting faculty bring. To date, over 75 professionals have completed IFC's training-of-trainers and are part of PICG's visiting faculty with skill sets ranging from extensive boardroom experience, legal, audit and accounting to bank governance, corporate secretarial, academia, human resources, and strategic management.

Over two years from September 2010 to December 2012 that the five-part programme was conducted, PICG had 23 intakes engaging 279 participants, of whom 205 attained certification. The completion percentage had increased significantly from 56 per cent in BDS to 73 per cent for CGLS.

PICG had been in discussion with SECP about accelerating director education as there were potentially over 4,000 directors of listed companies and banks and financial institutions that needed to be educated in good governance practices. SECP decided to make this a mandatory requirement through the stock exchanges. PICG had capacity limitations and was desirous of entering into partnerships with other professional bodies and institutions of higher learning. To enable this, it decided to make a major investment in e-learning tools.

The initiative taken was to make CGLS into a standardized

training product that could be franchised as an online, web-driven programme that provided pre-reading material and self-assessment tests as well as a comprehensive examination. PICG had again taken the lead among IFC's MENA region and to date, it remains the only director training institute that has enabled CGLS as an online, web-based product, thereby reducing the workshop attendance to merely four days. IFC, recognizing the efforts of PICG, agreed to provide its own accreditation to the Certificate of Director Education being issued by PICG at the end of such director education programmes.

PICG has introduced a Code of Conduct for visiting faculty as well as for the participants. This was necessary to professionalize the programme. Additionally, it has brought about changes to some of the topics that are addressed through the workshops as topics that are better addressed as on line pre-reading material. Such changes are pre-cleared by IFC as it is basically IFC's resource material that we use. Every year, PICG enters into a Technical Cooperation Agreement with IFC that authorizes such use. Over the past two years, PICG has also been authorized to use the highly specialized Bank Governance training programme developed by GCGF, primarily for MENA. As bank regulation in Pakistan is much better than the rest of MENA and next to none globally, PICG has localized this programme with the assistance of Hikmah Consulting, a leading banking consultants group. As this programme falls short of the mandatory certification requirement now being implemented by the Code of Corporate Governance 2012, PICG has developed an add-on one-day conversion programme that would lead to the Certificate in Director Education that is recognized by SECP for the mandatory certification requirement.

More recently, sensing the need of some senior executives to further reduce the time away from their work schedules when they come for director education, PICG has introduced a fast-track three-day programme involving longer hours each day but occupying the weekend. PICG also conducts for companies, especially groups of companies, an in-house director education programme that is dedicated to directors and senior executives of the group.

It has been interesting to note the mix of participants that have been encouraged to enter into director training. An analysis of the 480 participants who have attained the Certificate in Director Education shows that nearly 40 per cent were not mandatorily required to do so but have come into this to enhance their own knowledge and skills. Among these are third generation members of family-owned businesses, directors of private limited companies, and women in business. Regarding the latter, PICG is pioneering the drive for gender diversity on Boards and to date almost 10 per cent of the participants who have completed their certification are women.

In the same vein, it is also encouraging to note that Pakistani professionals, particularly in multinational companies, banks, and the large business houses with global operations are relocated to outside Pakistan and with progressively increasing responsibilities, are often placed on global Boards. PICG has taken the lead to enter into an affiliation with the Institute of Directors (IoD), UK, and offer IoD's Accelerated Certificate in Company Direction in Pakistan for those individuals who seek placement on global Boards.

Director education has come a long way since February 2007. Today, Pakistan is the only jurisdiction that mandates director certification and is being cited at international forums for doing so. It is heartening to note that other professional bodies and institutes of higher learning have also taken the step to conduct director training programmes. Hopefully, by June 30, 2016, and as desired by the SECP, every director on the Board of every listed company and all banks and financial institutions as well as non-banking finance companies would have completed the mandatory certification requirement or obtained exemption from SECP for doing so. In the process, hopefully, there will now be only a few heard to say, 'I have been a director for so many years. What are you going to teach me?'

CHRONOLOGY OF EVENTS

The Formative Years

Mar. 2002	Pakistan's Code of Corporate Governance implemented through the stock exchanges
Dec. 2004	PICG set up in public-private partnership for effective implementation of good corporate governance practices
June 2005	World Bank issues Report on the Observance of Standards and Codes (ROSC) on corporate governance in Pakistan

Aug. 2005	MoU between Securities Exchange Commission of Pakistan (SECP) and IFC on launch of Pakistan Corporate Governance Project (PCGP) and to enable PICG to: • build capacity • become commercially viable and • provide quality corporate governance services
May 2006	Conference on Corporate Governance in Banks held by State Bank of Pakistan in collaboration with PICG and IFC

The Fast Forward Years

Feb. 2007	Roll-out of Individual Director Training & Certification programme by PICG with PCGP collaboration
Apr. 2008	Cooperation Agreement between PICG and IFC for Board Development Series (BDS) director education Cooperation Agreement between PICG and IFC for developing curriculum of educational institutions
June 2009	Completion of PCGP Phase I
June 2010	PICG demonstrates sustainability
Feb. 2011	Cooperation Agreement between PICG and IFC for Corporate Governance Leadership Skills (CGLS) director education
Sep. 2011	Cooperation Agreement between PICG and IFC for Bank Governance supplement to CGLS

Apr. 2012	Revised Code of Corporate Governance 2012 implemented making many provisions mandatory, including director training
Apr. 2013	PICG identified as the lead institution for CSR and Sustainable Development initiatives as Responsible Business Conduct
Sep. 2013	Public Sector Companies (Corporate Governance) Rules 2013 implemented

Chapter 9

Assessing the Efficacy of Implementation

Arif Masud Mirza

Let us go straight to the very heart of this chapter and look at the governance metrics; what we have achieved in our regulatory journey from March 2002, the launch date of the original Code of Corporate Governance, to December 2014, a period of over 12 years.

The Code itself had a long gestation period in comparison with global trends, and this was followed by a painful birth. Back in 2002, the labour room was full of expectant fathers of industry, but the reaction to the rather underweight document was less than paternal; some fathers of the industry walked out of the labour room screaming 'regulatory murder'. Luckily the Code was not stillborn but left somewhat of an orphan. A decade later, many of those disappointed fathers have shown some fatherly feelings and the regulatory mother has delivered siblings: Code II and Code for Public Sector Enterprises.

During this decade, in which we have had one major revision to the original Code of Corporate Governance as promised by the apex stakeholder, the SECP at the time, we have seen the creation of the Pakistan Institute of Corporate Governance, the lead Corporate Governance education provider for company directors, leaders and executives of industry. PICG has trained over 500 directors and executives from over 300 companies of which approximately 135 are listed and would comprise the target group for the Code of Corporate Governance in terms of institutions. However, the more important figure would be the number of Board members trained by the PICG and here it is rather more difficult than to simply review the certified director list on the PICG website, because many companies designate their senior staff as directors without the latter necessarily being members of the Board of Directors. A quick desk count of the numbers shows approximately 340 designated as directors and 190 as non-directors. This is also indicative that companies are building directorial capacity for succession organically, which is good for the company and industry as a whole.

More recently, we have seen the launch of the Code of Corporate Governance for Public Sector Corporations (again a quick review of the PICG list of certified directors indicates that public sector companies like LESCO, TCPL stand out), as well as the launch of the voluntary Corporate Social Responsibility guidelines for listed companies. We also have a plethora of other peripheral guides and best practices from a range of stakeholders from the Accountancy profession to the State Bank of Pakistan. There have been numerous seminars, conferences, symposiums, workshops, round tables, square tables, task forces, standing committees, steering committees, and of course, orientations. These are all, in my opinion, a measure of the appetite for learning and developing in industry in Pakistan today. A Google search of such events will show that Pakistan is clearly several governance furlongs ahead in the region.

Figure 1: A breakdown of the PICG membership

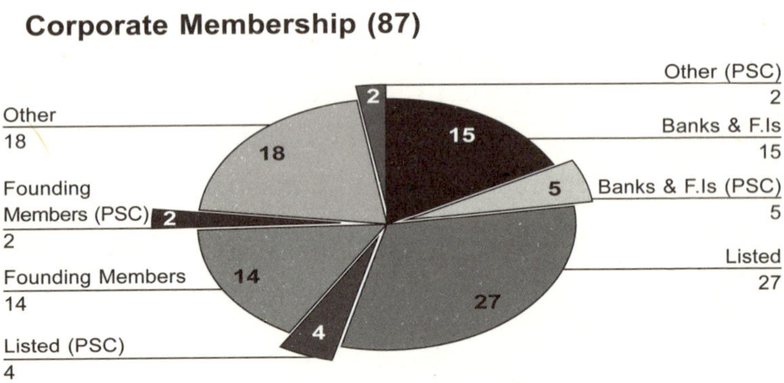

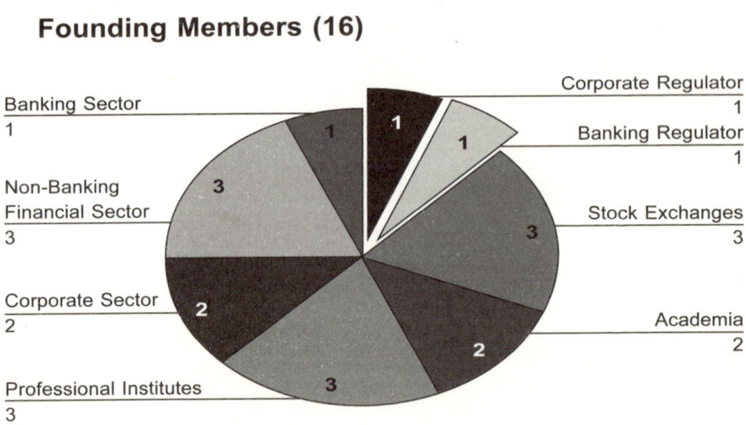

Figure 2: Participation in PICG initiatives

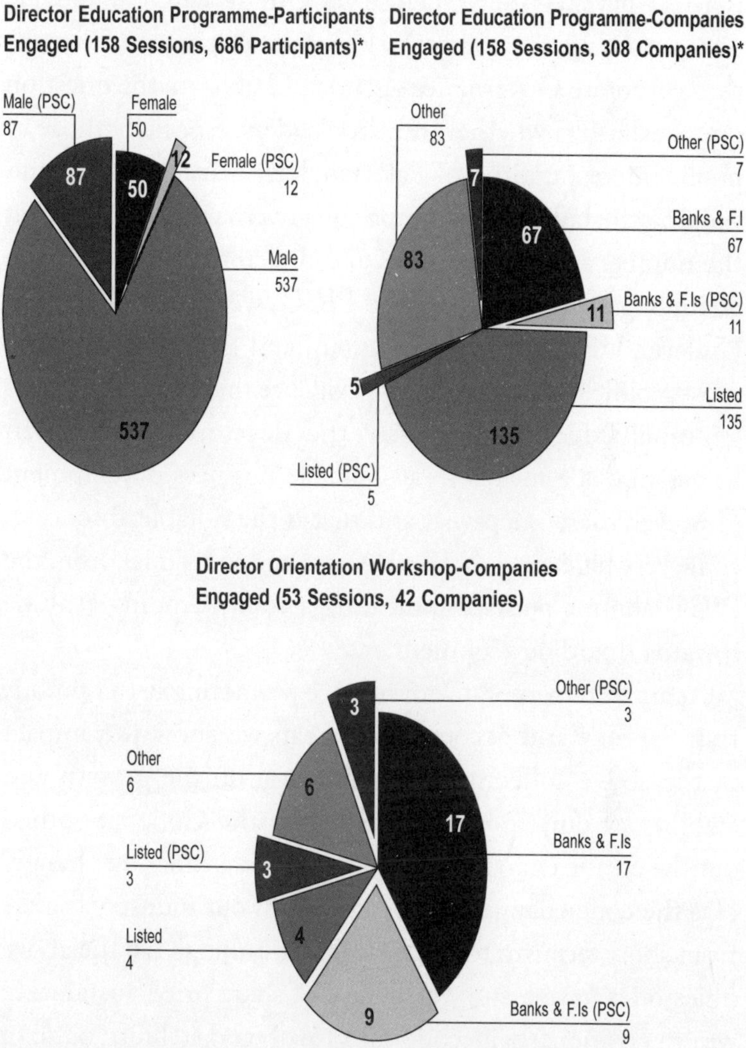

*2007 till date—468 participants (65 from PSCs and 275 from listed companies) have attained Certificate of Director Education of which 166 are from the PICG membership

Whilst national professional institutions (both ICAP and ICMAP have registered themselves with the SECP to provide director orientation courses) try to stake a claim on who owns the Corporate Governance agenda of Pakistan, the question one must ask is whether industry leaders, especially those of public interest entities of Pakistan, have started owning and walking the talk of good corporate governance. If we look at the number of top executives and directors of the KSE top 50 amongst the alumni of the PICG, we have to highlight Unilever, UBL, the Dawood group and Allied Bank as the most prolific. This is prima facie evidence that these companies genuinely do take seriously the development of their leadership as a means to sustainable business development. However, there is a caveat and that is the notable absence of some very big names, both corporate and individual, from the PICG alumni, perhaps indicating a condescending attitude towards Board development.

Apart from corporate governance promoting better probity, transparency and accountability, can we show the impact of the above collectively or singularly on the growth and stability of our capital markets? Has the Code smoothed out the erratic chartist path of our Karachi Stock Exchange? Has the code changed the behaviour of our industry leaders from short termism to strategic long thinking? Do the above milestones have a story to tell us, of share price, sustainable wealth creation, socioeconomic growth and stability, or all of the above?

Let us start with a favourite CG indicator, Board behaviour. The Code of Corporate Governance in 2002 and later in 2012 mandated orientation courses for Boards of Directors;

what the professional would call Continuous Professional Development, a term used by professional bodies to ensure that their members keep their knowledge and skills up to date, essentially to improve their directorial and management competence, but also and more importantly, from institutional and society optics to mitigate the risk of failing to remain up to date with technical and management advances, and changing legal and regulatory frameworks.

It seems perfectly sensible and a matter of principle to prescribe continuous learning to build capability and therefore individual and collective behaviour for those individuals who claim to lead our national industry. Directors are stewards of trillions of Rupees in capital value and are in the driving seat when it comes to steering enterprises that provide the public with goods, services and employment, navigating through increasing regulatory complexity, operating risks, and changing business models, not to mention mega forces such as climate change, natural resource scarcity, and urbanization, to name a few.

Let us look at the number of Boards that now have non-executive directors (NEDs), which is an indicator of greater openness and accountability of Board behaviour. Eighty-five per cent of KSE 100 companies say they have one to 10 non-executive directors (desk survey assisted by staff of Deloitte Pakistan 2014/15) compared to 65 per cent in 2007 (IFC: a survey of corporate governance practices in Pakistan 2007). The latter survey included the prefix 'independent' in its findings, but with the caveat that this was not understood by respondents who clubbed independent with non-independent. But let us take the rising percentage as a positive sign.

The number of companies that separated the role of Chairman from CEO: we see a high 95 per cent of KSE 100 companies that do segregate these important roles (desk CG survey assisted by staff of Deloitte Pakistan 2014/15) compared to 85 per cent in 2007 (IFC: a survey of corporate governance practices in Pakistan 2007).

The number of companies that had an NED to chair the audit committee, a mandatory committee of the Board in 2014/15: 97.5 per cent of KSE 100 had appointed a non-executive director to chair as well as 97.5 per cent affirming that a majority on this important committee are non-executive. Unfortunately, the term independent has been lost in the cloud of regulatory fog. Back in 2007, 95 per cent of those surveyed affirmed they had an audit committee with only 34 per cent claiming to have a majority of NEDs on this committee. So we see a healthy adoption: a 63.5 per cent increase in those companies, now tipping the balance of audit committee membership to the non-executives.

We may ask ourselves, 'Do we see any sustainable change in the long term capital investment inflows into our capital markets over the period 2002 to 2013 and how reasonable is it to accredit this to our improving regulatory frameworks?' The graph below tells us a very compelling story, which is certainly not one of sustainability. But a chartist will tell you that event certainly took a turn around the period of 2002; whether this was because of regulatory reforms, the leadership team at the time, etc, one can only guess. The dramatic fall from 2007 can be linked to the global financial crisis that spread around the world following the sub-prime mortgage collapse in the US.

Figure 3: Net foreign direct investment in Pakistan (total, US$)

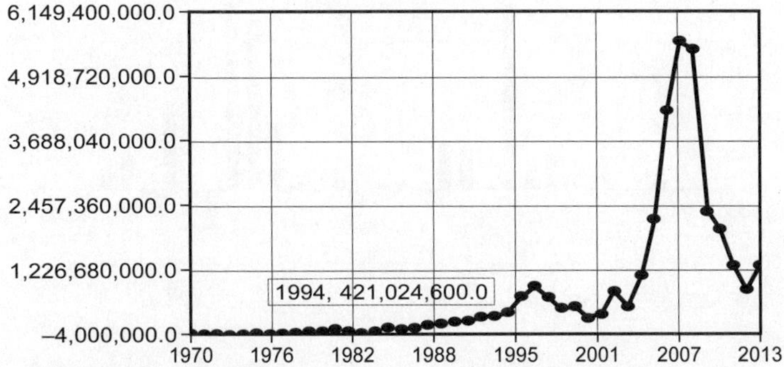

http://www.indexmundi.com/facts/pakistan/foreign-direct-investment

If we examine net portfolio investment over a similar period—and here the dependency is more on capital market regulatory frameworks and stability—again we see healthy investments immediately post–2002 and then a tapering off again, maybe due to the same reasons.

I am in no doubt that the introduction of corporate governance regulatory reforms combined with the mechanism of stakeholder education and strengthening the monitoring and evaluation function of the regulators has smoothed the working of our capital markets and indicators of our business performance, and our use of capital.

Wearing my auditor's hat, I have to qualify both the empirical evidence shared above as well as my experienced opinion, because there has been an elephant or two in the corporate governance room for the last ten years, that may have spoilt the chartist party; firstly, the war on terror being waged in our region which tends to distort and devour all

Figure 4: Pakistan net portfolio equity inflows

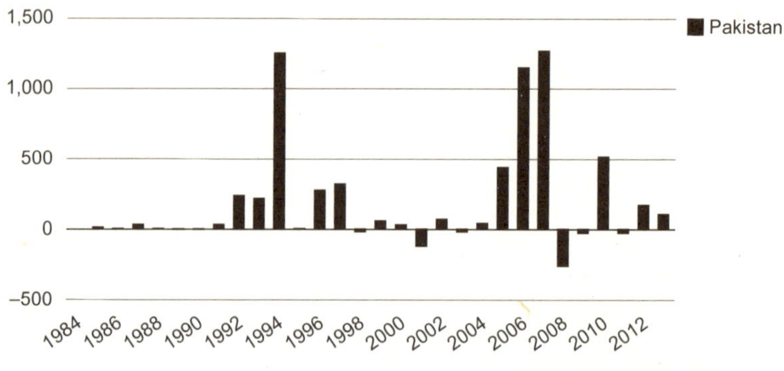

http://www.theglobaleconomy.com/Pakistan/Portfolio_investment_inflows/

other regulatory evolutionary steps to improve economic growth and secondly, the stop-go of democracy, including political governance; what one may term the flip side of the corporate governance coin.

Having governance codes is not a panacea for economic growth and stability, but combined with great leadership, political stability, robust regulators, a commitment to business ethics, and entrepreneurship, and a strong accountancy profession with independent audits, can play a compelling role in attracting investment for large capital projects and smoothing out economic progress.

One of the areas where we expected to see a transformation was in the creation of Board committees. Often the Board is overwhelmed by paperwork made extra complicated by the layers of bureaucracy created by regulators. The Code of Corporate Governance encouraged the formation of committees such as Audit Committees, HR Committees,

Risk Management Committees, and all these were to be chaired by Independent non-executive directors to exercise objective and arm's length oversight over the executive. 42.5 per cent of KSE 100 companies said they only had one independent director on their board, compared with eight per cent in 2007; 22.5 per cent had two, 7.5 per cent had three and 17.5 per cent had more than three independent directors. In comparison, in 2007, 44 per cent had 2–5 and 18 per cent had 6–10 independent directors. There was still a significant 10 per cent with no independent directors. The base bands were rather different in 2007: 23 per cent of responses with zero. With some confidence we may say that over the period more companies have appointed independent directors but we still have very opaque evidence on the weightage of independence on the listed company boards (Ref: desk CG survey assisted by staff of Deloitte Pakistan 2014/15 and IFC: a survey of corporate governance practices in Pakistan 2007).

How many companies have gone beyond the prescribed Pakistan doctrine and implemented other committees to enhance the levels of governance, such as forming nomination committees tasked with scouting for the best executive and leadership talent for the company and recommending the best candidates to the board for selection? Indeed, the nomination committee should also be looking at its own succession planning. There are numerous public interest companies at the moment without permanent leadership or with inadequate and incapable leadership simply because of a lack of application of corporate minds at the top.

One of the critical areas where Pakistan has been punching above its corporate governance weight has been in corporate sustainability and environmental reporting. No doubt the economy is a challenged one, facing massive energy shortages. Twelve years ago, the business community had been criticizing sustainability and environmental reporting as a bridge too far for our stage of economic development, but clearly the world places an immense importance on climate change and the impact business products, services and processes have on the planet, people and profitability. ACCA Pakistan and the World Wide Fund for Nature Pakistan (WWF) have been rewarding organizations that prepare and release sustainability and environmental reports for the last 12 years. The Awards now have over 50 entries each year of voluntary reports, many of which now comply with GRI standards. In 2013 the SECP, recognizing the global importance of the CSR agenda, issued its own voluntary CSR guidelines for listed companies to provide a start to best practices. Unfortunately, these guidelines are already out of date as the ESG agenda has moved beyond corporate philanthropy to sustainability and now towards integrated reporting. Nations are committing to ever lower impacts on climate change. This means lowering the carbon footprint of business processes, setting continuously challenging targets for greenhouse gas emissions as well as for water usage. We are also seeing a trend in a focus on human rights at the workplace, which means a scrutiny of gender, ethnic and race issues, child labour, and labour conditions generally. Global supply chains and a more interconnected world means that Pakistani companies are subject to global protocols and regulations and there is a high risk of sanctions, embargos and moratoriums if Board directors do not begin to appreciate the importance of these factors to the future survival and success of their businesses. By creating committees with expert members, the company will ensure that its present and future is being governed at the highest levels for future generations.

BOARD PERFORMANCE

What are the key performance indicators for collective Board performance and individual director performance? Both quantitative and qualitative measures should be used to strike the right balance. How much time did the Board spend on strategic planning, one of its core duties? Another area is risk management and nominations and selection of leading executives. At an individual level, how many times did directors speak during meetings? Did they ask questions on sensitive business issues? It is the responsibility of the chairman to periodically sit down with individual Board members to agree upon their key performance indicators and then provide feedback and review performance. According to the Zaffar Khan research of 2006 into Board behaviour, more than 50 per cent of responses indicated no process for Board performance measurement, either collectively or individually. Today, only 20 per cent of KSE 100 companies have in place a Board evaluation process; 75 per cent had no evident performance evaluation process (desk survey assisted by staff of Deloitte Pakistan 2014/15).

We must not forget that the Board is made up of human beings with diverse personalities and often formidable egos. Ensuring these testosterone charged men and women perform well as a team requires both empathetic and candid behavioural styles that need to be developed via day meetings, ice breaking activities, social interaction, and inspirational training.

It is also vital that the Board function as a team and that development needs be identified to build the capabilities of the Board members. This area has now been mandated by the SECP through the revised Code of Corporate Governance, with the leading role being played by the Pakistan Institute of Corporate Governance through their Board development series. The International Finance Corporation, one of the main international equity investors in Pakistan, has been an important pillar in institutionalizing the PICG and providing a framework for Board training and development. The current data says 92.5 per cent of KSE 100 companies have organized corporate governance orientations and training programmes for their Board members. This is rather an optimistic metric when compared with the earlier PICG snapshot. Back in 2007, we had only 77 per cent affirming Board development. Clearly, things have improved over the last seven years but there is a long way to go and we really need to improve the acquirement of quality data. More resources need to be put into the PICG to support its able leadership.

On reflection, there still remains a lack of ownership of the corporate governance agenda in Pakistan and increasingly the auditing profession is stepping into this 'trainer' space. This may have serious repercussions in reinforcing the box-ticking labelling of the corporate governance agenda and creating a culture of one size fits all, especially at the base of the pyramid. On the contrary, corporate governance is about behaviour at the top, which gives rise to the saying that a dead 'fish always rots from the head'. Stop the head from rotting and the rest of the functional parts will also stop rotting.

I don't believe that we can close the discussion on Board behaviour without having a closer look at the behaviour of the institutional Board members, i.e. Board members who represent institutional shareowners, and I use the term owners deliberately because there is a fundamental difference between share ownership and shareholding. Ownership brings with it the ultimate benefit of voting. Institutions like NIT, SLIC, and NBP have very large investment portfolios. However, their nominees on the Boards of many of Pakistan top corporations behave more like custodians of shares, i.e. passive rather than proactive sceptical significant share owners. Rarely do they play any important part in committees like the nomination and audit committees. Pakistan must continue to strive for robust reforms in its corporate legal frameworks, ensure talent management across the organizations, take the bold step of choosing professionals over coronation of incapable family members for important leadership positions; and lastly, regulators like the SECP, CCP, SBP, and the Professional Accountancy bodies must have moral courage.

Chapter 10

The Next Act: Women on Boards

Sadia Khan

INTRODUCTION

'It isn't so much what's on the table that matters, as what's in the chairs'.

Sir William Gilbert

No discourse on corporate governance would be complete without tackling the issue of gender diversity at the Board level. A number of misperceptions abound about the competence of women in reaching the highest level of the corporate hierarchy, as do myths about their own priorities in aspiring to those positions. There is a strong business case for the induction of more women on corporate Boards and this chapter attempts to draw international comparison with what currently persists in Pakistan, discussing some of the initiatives being taken worldwide and what makes sense in the local environment.

Globally, despite a 40 per cent representation in the workforce, women occupy only 12 per cent of positions at the Board level. The reasons for this steep corporate pyramid are well documented. Women face obstacles in the context of their respective environments, which may have to do with educational choices and traditional views and stereotypes about women. They face financial constraints in accessing formalized channels of finance, especially in countries where the financial system is highly collateralized. Women own fewer assets than men and are not helped by discriminatory inheritance laws. Finally, they encounter a number of soft obstacles, defined as the lack of adequate training, access to relevant networks, mentoring opportunities, and the lack of role models.

Figure 1: The talent gap

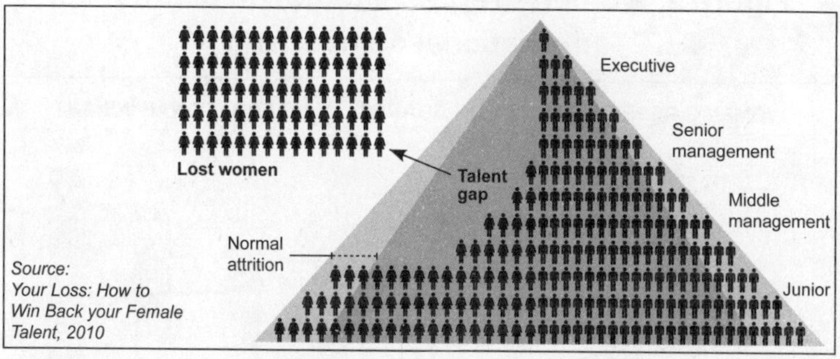

While a number of more progressive institutions have started dealing with these obstacles, their efforts are limited to those easiest to deal with, the soft targets. Mentoring opportunities, counselling and role models for women are much more common today than when I started my career 24 years ago. However, it is the contextual constraints that are the most limiting, but also by their very nature, the most difficult to deal with.

Changing the mindset of a generation about the role of women will probably take a generation, but only if we start now. Propagating it as their inherent right will not win over too many detractors. It is therefore more important to make a business case for more women in leadership positions.

1. INTERNATIONAL COMPARISON:

Figure 1 shows women's representation on Boards around the world. Norway leads the way with 34 per cent representation, followed by Sweden and Finland.

Figure 2: Women's representation on boards—an international comparison

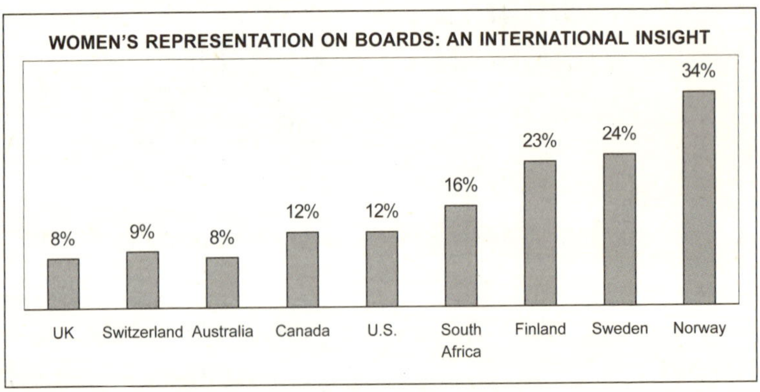

Source: 2012 data from Catalyst

Later in the chapter we will discuss some of the measures that these countries have taken to increase these figures over the past decade.

According to a women on Boards survey conducted in 2014 by MSCI Inc., the aggregate percentage of women on Boards is only 12.4 per cent. The percentage of companies with at least one female director stands at 63 per cent, though this figure goes down dramatically for companies with more than three female directors. The percentage of companies with a female chair is a dismal 3.5 per cent.

Table 1: International aggregate percentages of women on boards over time

Global Aggregate Percentages				
	Q4 2009	Q4 2010	Q4 2011	Q1 2013
Companies Analysed	4,233	4,205	4,028	4,332
Aggregate Percentage of women on boards (WOB)	9.30%	9.80%	10.50%	11.00%
Aggregate total directors	41,968	41,838	40,144	46,269
Aggregate total female directors	3,910	4,097	4,230	5,077
Per cent of companies with at least 1 female director	56.10%	58.20%	60.10%	62.50%
Per cent of companies with at least 3 female directors	8.30%	8.50%	10.10%	13.00%
Per cent of companies with a female chair	2.00%	2.20%	2.20%	2.30%

MSCI, Inc. Governance Issue Report. Women on Boards Survey, 2014

GMI Ratings' 2013 Women on Boards Survey: worldwide, women hold only 11 per cent of the Board seats despite 40 per cent representation in the global workforce (World Bank, 2013).

Table 2: Current levels of women on boards by region (as of November 2014)

Region	# of companies (2014)	% of women on boards	% of companies with at least 1 woman	% of companies with at least 3 women	% of companies with female chairs
Australia/ New Zealand	242	16.7	72.3	9.1	5.4
Industrialized Asia	613	3.5	27.4	2.1	1.0
Industrialized Europe	893	18.6	84.8	29.7	3.8
Nordic Countries	123	29.6	99.2	48.8	7.3
US/Canada	3,373	13.1	67.2	10.9	3.5
Americas	171	6.3	42.7	4.1	0.6
Emerging Asia	655	7.0	46.1	4.1	3.0
Emerging Europe	71	8.9	53.5	5.6	8.6
Middle East and Africa	178	15.1	78.1	21.3	6.2
Tax Havens	247	10.3	56.7	8.1	2.4
Global	6,566	12.4	63.7	12.5	3.5
Global Ex-IndEur/ Nordic	5,550	10.9	59.5	9.0	3.2

MSCI, Inc. Governance Issue Report. Women on Boards Survey, 2014

On a regional basis, the Nordic countries lead the way with an average of 29.6 per cent female representation on Boards, followed by industrialized Europe and Australia/New Zealand.

Industrialized Asia ranks lowest in this list with a 3.5 per cent representation. It is interesting to note that even in the case of the Nordic countries, the percentage of companies with more than three women directors is significantly lower than those with just one female director. The number of companies with female chairs is also noticeably low for these same countries.

A comparison across Board representation and executive committee representation also produces interesting figures. In 2013, while Norway boasted a 34 per cent Board representation of women, their representation on executive committees was only 14 per cent. This is perhaps indicative of the kind of measures that have been put in place in these countries to catapult women to more senior positions despite the lack of a commensurate build up in the corporate pipeline.

Figure 3: Women's representation at the top levels of corporations

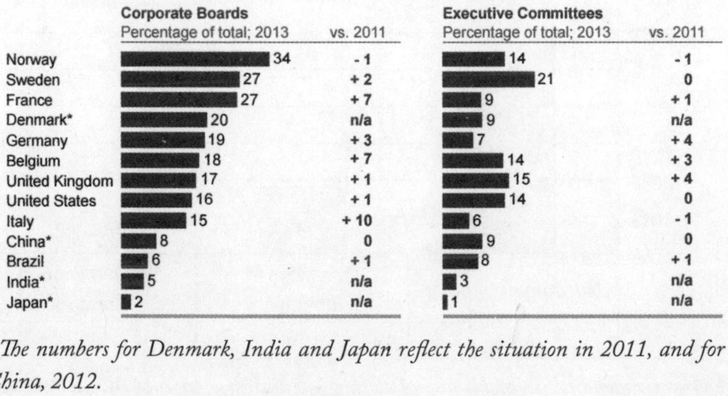

** The numbers for Denmark, India and Japan reflect the situation in 2011, and for China, 2012.*

Source: Company websites, McKinsey analysis

PAKISTAN'S EXPERIENCE

In Pakistan's case, not enough focus has been given to the issue of gender diversity at the Board level. In the revised Code of Corporate Governance, while the section on Board composition includes gender diversity as a desirable objective, it falls short of recommending any specific measures. The data below speaks for itself. Women representation on Boards in Pakistan is largely within the family-owned businesses where they are inducted more for filial affiliation than their professional worth. This comes out strongly in the chart depicting criteria for Board nomination where qualification and professional experience rank low in comparison to family relationships.

Figure 4: Women's representation on boards in Pakistan

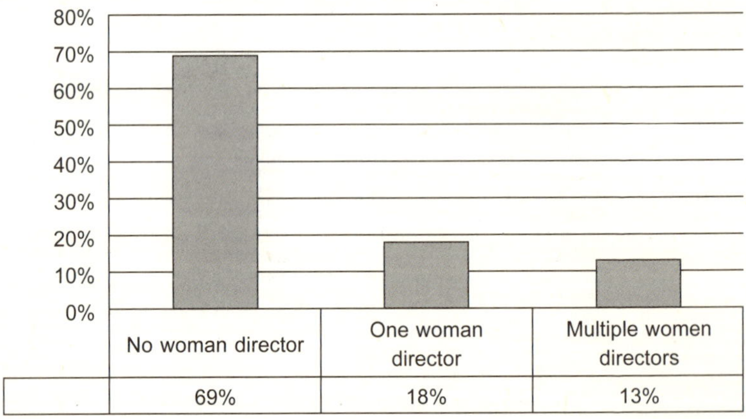

Source: Gender diversity on boards in Pakistan—A discussion paper by ACCA Pakistan, June 2010

Figure 5: Women's representation on boards by company ownership

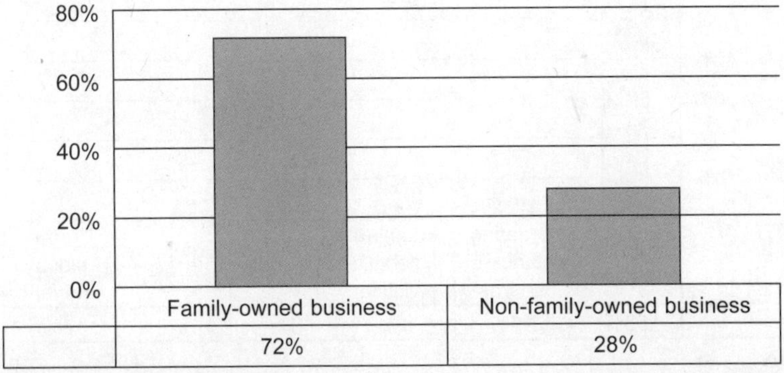

Source: Gender diversity on boards in Pakistan—A discussion paper by ACCA Pakistan, June 2010

Figure 6: Women's representation on boards of KSE 100 index companies

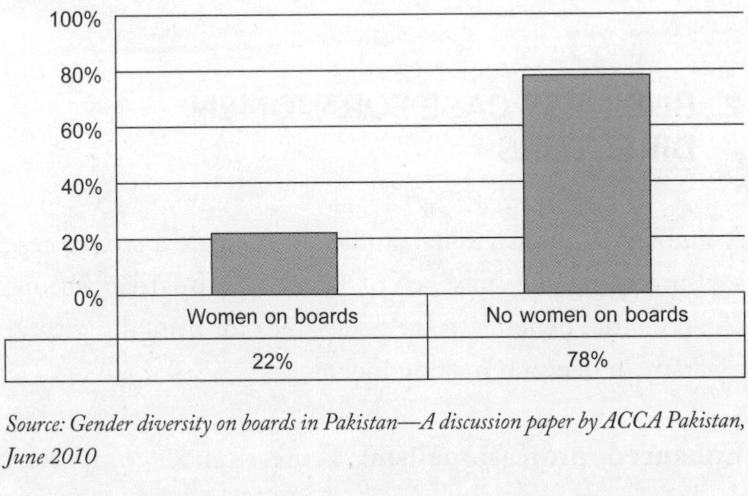

Source: Gender diversity on boards in Pakistan—A discussion paper by ACCA Pakistan, June 2010

Figure 7: Criteria for board nomination/appointment of women

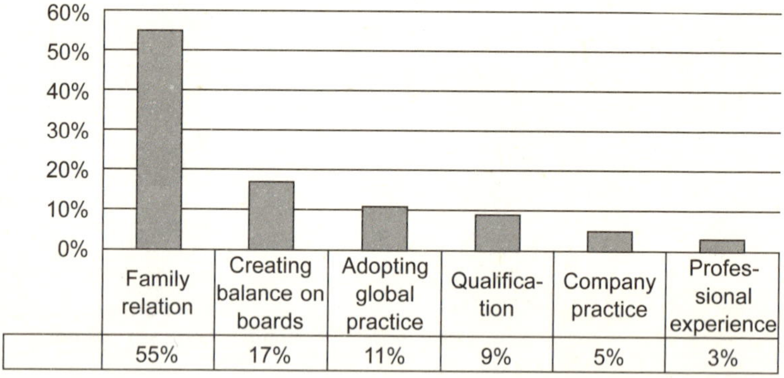

Source: Gender diversity on boards in Pakistan—A discussion paper by ACCA Pakistan, June 2010

According to the Survey on Board Practices in Pakistan 2011, conducted by the Pakistan Institute of Corporate Governance, only 22 per cent of the 59 companies that responded to the questions 'feel that (the) presence of women on the Board of Directors adds value to the Board.'

2. BUSINESS CASE FOR WOMEN DIRECTORS

A number of international studies have made a strong case for increasing the presence of women in Board positions. The potential benefits to the companies for bringing greater diversity in decision making include:

Enhanced professionalism: Professional, competent,

experienced and knowledgeable women bring a different dimension to managerial deliberations leading to enhanced strategic formulation for the benefit of the company. Diversity in the boardroom results in innovative thinking, more objective discussion, improved governance, greater ethical consciousness, more diversity in point of view, more appropriate allocation of budget, and better decisions, which will lead to better financial performance.

More responsive to the market: Women are responsible for 70 per cent of household purchasing decisions. Their presence in the corporate hierarchy ensures that there is an improved understanding of customer needs and more informed decision making.

Diversity of opinions, experiences, competencies and skills on boards results in effective and balanced board decisions, efficient oversight of financial management and enhanced accountability to shareholders.

Better corporate governance: Women bring a greater ethical consciousness to the workplace and their focus on non-financial performance ensures the company remains cognizant of its social responsibilities as well.

'Multiple academic studies have concluded that diverse Boards exercise more diligent oversight. They have better attendance records than homogenous Boards, and they invest more effort in auditing when the complexity of the business warrants heightened scrutiny,' says Michelle Lamb.

Improved company performance: Diversity of skills

and enhanced accountability lead to improved financial performance. Net income growth of companies having women on the Board is more as compared to all-male Boards. Companies with more women on their Boards were found to outperform their rivals and have more stable share prices. Empirical evidence collected subsequent to the 2008 economic downturn suggests that companies with more women on Boards/executive management consistently outperformed their rivals in terms of return on equity, return on sales and return on invested capital. In 2012, Credit Suisse Research Institute analysed the performance of almost 2,400 global companies and found that 'the average Return of Equity (ROE) of companies with at least one woman on the Board over a six year period (2008–12) was 16 per cent compared with companies with no female representation, 12 per cent'. Catalyst analysis revealed that on average Fortune 500 companies with more women directors had significantly higher measures of financial performance than those with the least; 53 per cent higher ROE, 42 per cent higher Return on Sales, and 66 per cent higher return on invested capital.

'Companies with women on Boards really outperformed when the downturn came through in 2008. Stocks of companies with women on Boards tend to be a little more risk averse and have on average a little less debt, which seems to be one of the key reasons why they've outperformed so strongly in this particular period,' says Mary Curtis.

These are strong and valid arguments, but how does one bridge the gap between awareness creation and concrete action? A number of countries around the world have instituted quotas for the percentage of women they would like to see serve at the highest levels of corporate hierarchy.

INITIATIVES TAKEN BY DIFFERENT COUNTRIES

The Nordic countries, including Norway, Finland, and Sweden are leading the way with a female representation at the Board level of 35.5 per cent for Norway and close to 30 per cent for both Finland and Sweden. However, while Norway has made its quota mandatory and made the use of legal instruments to increase female Board participation, several other countries in the European Union and others like Finland and Sweden have left it as a voluntary provision for their corporate sector to follow.

CHRONOLOGY OF WORLDWIDE INITIATIVES:

- Israel was the first country to pass a law in April 1999 requiring at least one woman on the Board of publicly traded companies.
- In 2003, Norway was the first country to introduce 'Board Gender Quotas': 40 per cent for all private listed companies. Norway tops the ranking of 20 countries across three regions, with 35.5 per cent female representation on the Boards of its listed companies.
- In 2007, Spain approved a quota for publicly traded

companies employing more than 250 workers to reach 40 per cent by 2015.

- In 2010, Iceland imposed a quota of 40 per cent for SOEs with at least 50 employees by 2013.
- In 2011, France set a quota of 20 per cent by 2014 and 40 per cent by 2017. Applicable to all listed/ unlisted companies employing at least 500 workers with revenues over Euros 50 million. Severe sanctions otherwise. Is currently far ahead of its 20 per cent interim target with women accounting for 29.7 per cent of Board seats, closing in on Finland's 29.9 per cent.
- In 2011, Netherlands imposed a 30 per cent quota to be achieved by 2016.
- In 2011, Belgium announced a target of 30 per cent by 2018. Currently has 23.4 per cent female representation on its Boards.
- In Italy, a gender quota of 33 per cent by 2015.
- Germany recently passed a law on quotas for women on company Boards. Germany's biggest companies have been ordered to ensure that 30 per cent of supervisory Board positions are held by women from 2016.

Countries with mandatory provisions/quotas:

- Norway (40 per cent)
- France (40 per cent by 2017)
- Spain (40 per cent by 2015)
- Iceland (40 per cent)

- Italy (33 per cent by 2015)
- Malaysia (30 per cent by 2016)
- Israel (at least one woman)
- India (at least one woman)
- Belgium (30 per cent by 2018)
- Netherlands (30 per cent by 2016)
- Germany (30 per cent by 2016)

Countries with voluntary/comply or explain provisions:

- Sweden
- Finland
- United Kingdom
- New Zealand
- Hong Kong
- Australia
- Denmark
- United States
- Canada
- South Africa

To see the impact of these measures, a comparison with France, which instituted quotas and the US, which has left it a voluntary provision, is made below. As can be seen, for the period 2004–14, France has made rapid gains, overtaking the US in the years after the measures were introduced. In the following comparison, again it is obvious that where stricter measures are in place, the gains have been more obvious in the past decade.

Figure 8: Percentage of women board directors of Fortune Global 200 companies in the U.S.A. and France, 2004–14

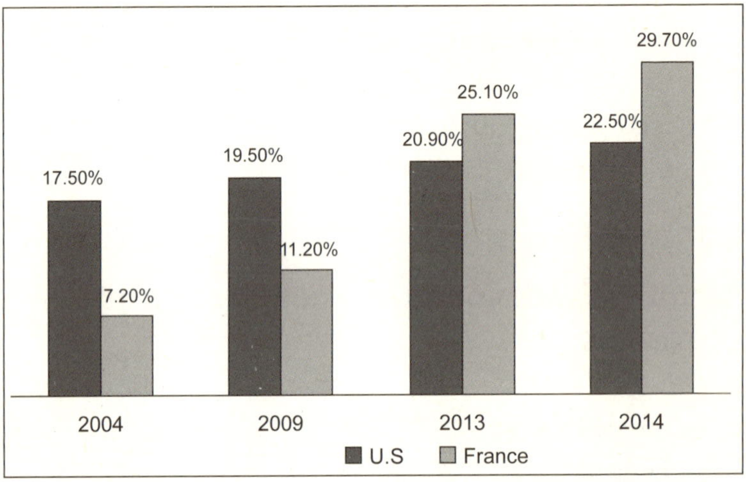

Source: 2014 CWDI Report – Women Board Directors of Fortune Global 200, 2004–14

Figure 9: Percentage change of women board directors of Fortune Global 200 companies, 2004–14

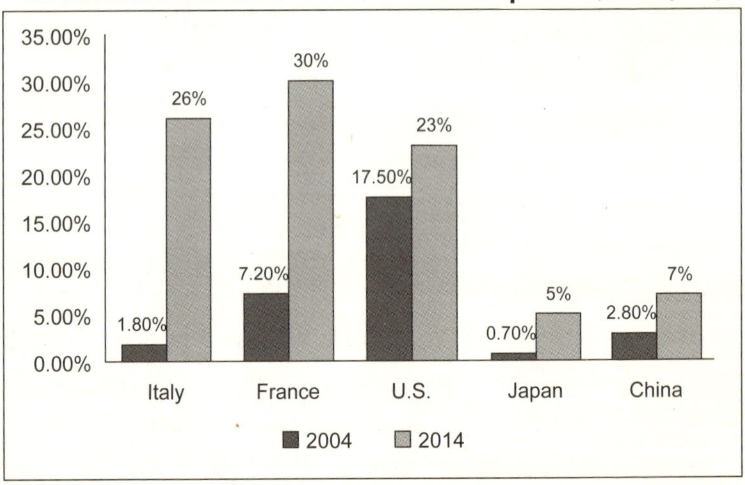

Source: 2014 CWDI Report – Women Board Directors of Fortune Global 200, 2004–14

Figure 10: Women directors in countries with quota legislation versus women directors at all Fortune Global 200 companies

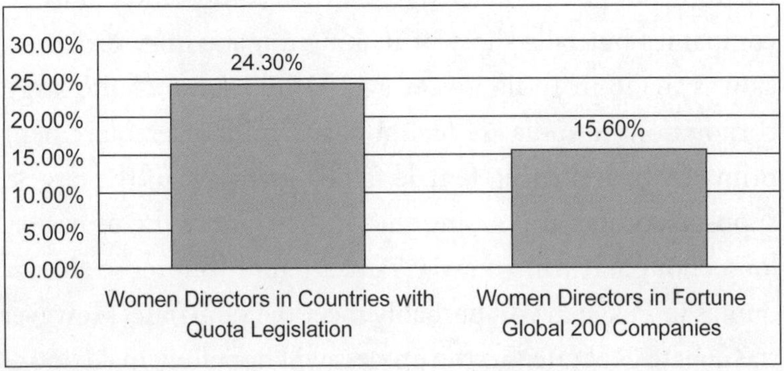

Source: 2014 CWDI Report – Women Board Directors of Fortune Global 200, 2004–14

In the final chart, women directors in countries with quotas stand at 24.3 per cent compared to women directors in all Fortune Global 200 companies, which stands at 15.6 per cent.

THE WAY FORWARD

While the gains made by countries who have taken measures over the past decade to facilitate the induction of more women on Boards has been immediate and obvious, it must be remembered that these same countries have had a longer tradition of female empowerment, persistent advocacy of equalitarian policies, and acceptance of the economic contribution of women to their respective economies. More groundwork needs to be done in Asia in general to change perceptions about the role of women in society and the economy, and shatter the myths surrounding their competencies.

The revised Code of Corporate Governance in Pakistan recommends gender diversity for Board composition of listed companies but falls short of making a mandatory provision as was made in India a year ago. While some of the large corporations in India are scrambling to fulfil this requirement, primarily by inducting female family members of the largest sponsors, others are hoping that if they ignore the provision long enough, it will go away. Any attempt to impose similar quotas in Pakistan will probably meet the same fate. However, the debate generated in the process will hopefully make more companies aware of the business case for inducting senior women in their hierarchy and prompt them to take action in their own long term interests.

The women themselves have to be at the forefront of this debate. Quotas have increased the need for women to have the appropriate set of corporate skills and relevant experience in order to facilitate their recruitment on Boards. The initiative to get the appropriate certifications, building up their portfolios, and making it part of their career aspirations lies with the women themselves, but with the appropriate backing of the men who need to champion their cause as the decision makers today. Once in a position to make a change, these women need to cherish their diversity as an asset on any Board and most importantly continue to advocate the cause for the next generation. They will have to pave the way for others to follow, ensuring that decision making is in the hands of a diverse group of innovative minds that not only improves shareholder value but makes this world a better place.

Bibliography

Akhtar, S., Virtanen, O. and Shah, A. A. Presentations at the Corporate Governance Conference (Karachi, 11 Apr. 2012) <http://picg.org.pk/wp-content/uploads/2015/11/Presentations-Governance-and-Board-Effectiveness-in-Public-Sector-Enterprises-April11-2012.pdf> Accessed in August 2016.

Balakrishnan, A. 'The New Guidelines on SOE Corporate Governance in India', [transcript] (25 Jun. 2008), <http://unpan1.un.org/intradoc/groups/public/documents/apcity/unpan048470.pdf> Accessed in August 2016.

Crown Company Monitoring Advisory Unit, *Owner's Expectations Manual for State-Owned Enterprises* (Wellington, 2007).

Dawood, A. R. 'Addressing Problems that Tear Families Apart: Why Good Governance Matters for Family Firms', *Centre for International Private Enterprise: Economic Reform Feature Service* (Washington, DC, 2007).

International Federation of Accountants, *Governance in the Public Sector* (New York, 2001).

Jaffer, M. J. and Sohail, S. B. 'Corporate Governance Issues in Family-Owned Enterprises', *Centre for International Private Enterprise: Economic Reform Feature Service* (Washington, DC, 2007).

Organisation for Economic Co-operation and Development, *OECD Guidelines on Corporate Governance of State-Owned Enterprises* (Paris, 2005).

———, *Policy Brief on Corporate Governance of State-Owned*

Enterprises in Asia (Paris, 2010).

Securities and Exchange Commission of Pakistan, *Code of Corporate Governance 2012* (Islamabad, 2012).

South Asian Federation of Accountants, *Best Practices on Corporate Governance for South Asian Countries* (2005). <http://www.icap.org.pk/wp-content/uploads/mies/mies8.pdf> accessed August 2016

Tan, L-H and Wang, J. 'Modelling an Effective Corporate Governance System for China's Listed State-Owned Enterprises: Issues and Challenges in a Transitional Economy', *Journal of Corporate Law Studies,* 7(2007), 143-183.

The Center for International Private Enterprise — Pakistan Office. *The Corporate Governance Guide: Family-Owned Companies* (Karachi, 2008).

———, *Safeguarding the Legacy: Corporate Governance and Longevity in Family-Owned Enterprises* (Karachi, 2011).

Wickaksono, A. 'Corporate Governance of State-Owned Enterprises: Investment Holding Structure of Government-Linked Companies in Singapore and Malaysia and Applicability for Indonesian State-Owned Enterprises', PhD dissertation, Universität St. Gallen (2007).

Wong, S. C. Y. 'Improving Corporate Governance in SOEs: An Integrated Approach', *Corporate Governance International,* 7 (2004), 5-15.

Index

A

academia 3, 199–200, 208, 229
ACCA 216, 225–8
accountability 6, 9–10, 15, 30–4, 37, 41, 44–50, 59–63, 67, 70, 74, 77, 88, 92, 98, 101, 106, 145, 152, 155–8, 166, 183–4, 210–11, 229–30
accounting 4–8, 11–12, 18, 24–5, 45, 55, 58, 70, 74, 103, 106, 111, 114–19, 128, 133–45, 152, 156, 164, 174, 180–1, 200, 207, 214, 219, 232, 237–8
accreditation 199–201, 212
activism 106, 158
advising 44, 77, 80–1, 93, 96, 106, 148, 151, 237
advocacy 5, 235–6
affiliation 81–2, 202, 226
agencies 114–15, 158, 160, 177, 180–2, 189
allocation 62, 92, 97, 101–2, 229
amendments 50, 89, 92–5, 103, 131–2, 143, 156–7, 161, 183
analysis 12, 37, 48, 61, 65, 85, 90–8, 107–8, 202, 223, 225, 230
assets 17, 31, 38, 71, 87, 93, 100, 114, 127, 128, 132, 134, 136, 193, 221, 236
auditing 7, 15–16, 21–2, 31–3, 42, 49, 54–6, 81–3, 88, 92–5, 99–106, 109, 112–15, 119–120, 131–45, 152, 156–8, 164, 174, 183–4, 200, 212–14, 218–19, 229
Australia 12, 222–4, 233
authority 22, 26, 41, 51, 56, 87, 93, 100, 130, 146, 161–2, 171, 176, 180–2, 188–9, 201

B

banking 8, 17, 19, 76, 79, 113–15, 119, 123, 129, 136–8, 140–1, 144, 150, 169, 193, 200–4, 208–9
Board Audit Committee (BAC) 93, 94
Board of Directors 6–10, 13–14, 20–34, 41–110, 113, 119–20, 131–9, 144–50, 153–4, 157–65, 178, 183–9, 193, 197–204, 207, 210–36
borrowing 38, 71, 121–4, 170–1, 180
bureaucracy 62, 214
business acumen 10, 73
business development 210
business environment 108–9, 157–8
business expansion 119

business judgment 10, 74, 81
business operations 99, 146

C

capacity 12, 16, 34, 38–9, 59, 131, 150, 189, 197, 200, 204, 207
capital expenditure 88, 97, 104, 186
capital management 38, 43
capital market 3–4, 26, 122, 210, 213
certification 34, 55–6, 199–204, 207, 236
chairman 6–7, 21, 24, 28–33, 47–51, 56, 98, 132–6, 150, 156, 161, 184, 212, 217, 220, 224–5
chambers (of commerce) 17–18, 25
Chartered Accountants 4–7, 18, 24–5, 34, 85, 115, 139–44, 158, 181, 210, 238
Chief Executive Officer (CEO) 13, 29–31, 44, 49–51, 54, 61–3, 77–8, 120, 131, 134–5, 145, 147, 150, 212
Chief Financial Officer (CFO) 33, 56, 120, 131, 134–6, 143, 145, 156
China 46, 225, 234, 238
code of best practices 3, 6, 11
code of conduct 53, 90, 94, 201
Code of Corporate Governance (CCG) 4, 16–24, 27, 37, 50, 64–5, 70, 86, 109, 113, 117, 131–2, 141–3, 153–7, 160–1, 198, 201–6, 210, 214, 218, 226, 236, 238
code of ethics 12, 53, 144
committees 6–13, 18, 21–2, 31–2, 47–9, 53–60, 64–6, 71, 82–6, 90–103, 109, 119, 129–38, 143–4, 156, 184, 187, 207, 212–19, 225
company boards 32, 215, 232
company law 5, 9, 27, 185–6, 193, 198
Companies Ordinance, 1984 74, 81, 116–17, 140–2, 160
company secretary 33, 56–7, 96–8, 120, 134
compensation 61, 84, 148, 154, 177
competence 12, 41, 60, 66, 69, 73–4, 82, 86, 90–2, 108, 149, 183, 211, 220, 228–9, 236
competition 10, 16, 43, 59, 91, 146, 158, 162, 181–2
Competition Commission of Pakistan (CCP) 182, 219
compliance 9, 12–13, 16, 24, 34, 48–50, 61–6, 71, 85–8, 93–6, 103–5, 108, 113, 130, 133–4, 137–8, 147, 156–7, 183, 198–9
consulting 24, 27–9, 32, 66, 77, 81–6, 93–4, 98–9, 101–3, 134, 137, 169, 201
contingency 126, 130
corporate affairs 156, 184
corporate failures 25, 27, 106
corporate governance 1–13, 19, 20–9, 34–7, 40–50, 58–61, 64–6, 70, 80, 85–94, 98–9, 106–10, 113–17, 132–65, 183–5, 197–9, 201–15, 218, 220, 226–9, 236–8
corporate hierarchy 220, 229–31
corporate law 180, 185, 192–3, 238

corporate sector 4, 8, 12, 16, 19, 35, 89, 108, 152, 158, 161–2, 178–82, 185, 198, 208, 231
Corporate Governance Leadership Skills (CGLS) 199–201, 204
Corporate Public Sector Enterprises (CPSES) 48–9
Corporate Social Responsibility (CSR) 91, 105, 205, 216
corruption 37–8, 54, 131–3, 155–8
credit 129, 146, 158, 161, 169–70, 185, 188, 199, 230
Crown Company Monitoring Advisory Unit (CCMAU) 44, 47, 60

D

debenture 121–23
debt 38–9, 104–5, 120, 124, 170, 230
democracy 10, 160–1, 185, 214
Development Finance Institution (DFI) 17, 76, 81–2, 140
directors 20–4, 29–30, 33–4, 50–2, 56–7, 71, 76–84, 90, 119, 131–2, 140, 145, 153, 156, 163, 171–3, 174, 179, 186–9, 190–1, 197–212, 215–17, 223–6
director education 197– 204, 209
director orientation 209–10
director training 33, 56, 199–205
see also independent directors, non-executive directors
Discounted Cash Flows method (DCF) 127, 129
divestment 16, 41, 179
dividends 104, 113, 117–18, 121–7, 164

E

earnings 105, 121–8
economy 8, 25–6, 36, 58, 65, 152, 155–7, 182, 216, 235–8
education 25, 56, 74, 91, 197–209, 213, 221
efficiency 33, 46, 51–2, 59, 69, 71, 93, 111, 152, 182, 229
employees 33, 39, 42, 53, 71, 80–1, 100, 120, 131, 140, 154, 189, 211, 232
entrepreneurship 10, 214
environmental 91, 147, 152, 155, 216
evaluation 32–3, 42, 49, 50–2, 56, 61, 65, 71, 85, 92–4, 97–100, 184, 199, 213, 217
executives 6, 13, 20, 29, 51–3, 70, 77–84, 88, 95, 98, 104, 119, 120, 137, 163–5, 174, 183–4, 186, 190–1, 202, 207, 210, 215–17, 221, 225, 230

F

family 13, 26, 79, 80–1, 153–4, 180, 193, 202, 219, 226–8, 236–8
financial crisis 107–8, 121, 145–6, 212

financial institutions 60, 62, 79, 104, 114–15, 123, 148–9, 156, 169, 200, 203
financial markets 110–11, 152
financial performance 38, 59, 61, 63, 88, 98, 110, 229–30
financial reporting 5, 6, 22, 71, 80, 93, 110–15, 118, 138
financial sector 73, 141, 144
financial statements 15, 55, 70–1, 88, 95, 104, 107, 111–18, 133, 136, 139, 158
Finland 37, 45, 47, 58, 222, 231–3

G

Germany 232–3
Global Corporate Governance Forum (GCGF) 198–201
government 16–17, 34, 37–41, 45–7, 51, 55, 58–60, 64–6, 114–15, 126, 147, 157, 180, 185, 238
Gross Domestic Product (GDP) 37, 45
guidelines 25–6, 31, 37, 40–2, 48–50, 60–1, 69, 143–4, 207, 216, 237

H

hierarchy 220, 229–31, 236

I

ICAP, *see* Chartered Accountants
ICMAP, *see* Chartered Accountants
implementation 7, 24–5, 37, 41–2, 48–54, 58–60, 63–6, 85–92, 96, 99, 108, 118, 131, 139, 182, 195, 197, 201–6, 215
in-house 76, 108, 202
independent directors 10, 20, 29, 30, 50–1, 78–82, 132, 152–6, 183, 215
India 37, 48–9, 60, 160, 177, 190, 225, 233, 236–7
Institutional Shareholders Services (ISS) 199
International Federation of Accountants (IFAC) 12, 142–4
International Finance Corporation (IFC) 86, 197–201, 204, 211–12, 215
investing 18, 36, 41, 43, 76, 104, 110–11, 119, 161, 165, 170–2, 191, 200, 212–14, 219, 238
Italy 232, 234

J

Japan 71–2, 225, 234
judiciary 12, 16, 162, 178, 185
jurisdiction 3–5, 11, 41, 50, 106–7, 158, 203

K

Karachi 4, 7, 18, 28, 161, 176, 179, 186, 189–93, 210, 237–8
Karachi Stock Exchange (KSE) 210–12, 215–18, 227

Key Performance Indicators (KPIs) 96–7

L

Lahore 18, 28, 161–3, 179, 186, 189
laws 5, 9, 12, 16, 26–7, 33–4, 52, 101, 107–8, 142, 161–3, 167, 171–5, 178, 179–81, 185–8, 191–3, 198, 221, 231–2, 238
leadership 51, 56, 74, 77, 82, 87, 98, 100, 108, 150, 181, 199, 204, 210, 212–15, 218–19, 222
legal 7, 12, 23, 40, 47–8, 58, 64–6, 79, 80–1, 88, 95, 104, 110, 116, 129, 147, 150, 167, 184–5, 191, 200, 211, 219, 231
legislation 9, 74, 103, 145, 160, 175–7, 182, 187, 235

M

Malaysia 37, 43, 47, 233, 238
management 6, 11–18, 22, 30–1, 38–44, 51, 54–63, 69, 74–8, 83, 88–95, 99–105, 108–9, 117, 122–6, 133, 137–9, 144–52, 159, 163–70, 176–9, 185, 200, 211, 215, 217–19, 221, 229–30
manpower 100
manufacturers 113, 190–3
market 3–4, 25–7, 38, 40, 59, 61, 80, 83, 106, 112, 122–3, 126–30, 145–6, 149, 152, 175, 181–2, 191, 213, 229
minority 10, 13–16, 104, 154, 161, 165–8, 176–85, 188, 192
mismanagement 76, 93, 178–9
modaraba 17–18, 120, 144
monitoring 15–16, 41–4, 48, 58–64, 71, 78, 85–6, 90–4, 101, 106, 118, 130, 134, 138–9, 149, 158, 174, 213, 237
Monopoly Control Authority (MCA) 162, 182

N

Netherlands, The 11, 232–3
New Zealand 37, 44, 47, 60, 224, 233
non-executive directors (NEDs) 6, 10, 13, 20–1, 45–7, 56, 70, 77–84, 98, 104, 132, 153–6, 179, 183–4, 211–12, 215

O

Organisation for Economic Cooperation and Development (OECD) 11, 40–1, 80, 107–8, 110–12, 237
ownership 5, 13, 15, 19, 26, 34–8, 40–1, 45–8, 58–65, 87, 110–11, 121, 152–3, 164, 174, 193, 210, 218–19, 227, 237

P

Pakistan Corporate Governance Project (PCGP) 197, 204

Pakistan Institute of Corporate Governance (PICG) 25–7, 34, 86, 197–210, 218, 237
parliament 45–7, 63, 85
penalties 107, 174–5
performance 32, 36–8, 42–4, 48–52, 56–65, 69–70, 75, 78, 85–99, 109–10, 146–8, 157–9, 184, 213, 217, 229, 230
professionalism 86, 201, 228
public enterprises 37–50, 57–66, 73, 112–16
public interest 14, 158, 166, 210, 215
public sector 34–7, 48, 64–6, 119, 141, 205–7

Q

quotas 231–36

R

records 70, 114–16, 150, 229
regulations 3–9, 12, 16, 19, 23, 40, 46, 50, 57–9, 62, 79, 88–90, 93–5, 104–8, 112, 116, 133, 137, 144–5, 147, 151, 155–62, 178–85, 198, 201, 206–8, 211–19
remuneration 14–15, 22, 31–3, 56–63, 78, 80–3, 107, 139–41, 145–9, 154
Report on the Observance of Standards and Codes (ROSC) 197, 203
resources 20, 31, 52, 59, 62, 92, 100–3, 133, 137–8, 157, 200–1, 211, 218
revenue 82, 95, 97, 113, 124, 146, 158, 232
risks 22, 42, 56, 74–8, 83, 90, 93–4, 99–109, 119, 129, 139, 145–50, 159, 199, 211, 215–17, 230

S

safeguards 9, 10, 23, 38, 52, 71, 87, 93, 99, 132, 136, 176–78, 183, 238
sanctions 71, 186, 216, 232
Sarbanes-Oxley Act 106, 151–2
Securities and Exchange Commission of Pakistan (SECP) 5–9, 18–19, 24–9, 32–3, 66, 104, 112–14, 141, 152, 155–8, 161, 171–5, 181–5, 188, 190–2, 197, 200–6, 210, 216–19
shareholders 13–17, 26, 29, 32–4, 40–3, 47–8, 51–9, 69–73, 80–4, 87–8, 93–4, 99, 102, 104, 110–16, 119–27, 136, 139–41, 147–8, 150–4, 161–92, 199, 219, 229, 236
Spain 231–2
sponsors 13, 26, 30, 34, 81, 174, 236
stakeholders 4–11, 17, 19, 23, 26–9, 32, 35, 40, 48, 55, 70, 75, 110, 116, 145, 151, 154–5, 160–2, 178, 183–5, 206–7, 213

State Bank of Pakistan 19, 73, 76, 79, 81, 82, 115, 136, 140–1, 204, 207, 219
Steering Committee for Public Sector Enterprises (SCPSE) 60–4
stewardship 21, 70, 87, 106, 157, 164, 211
stock exchanges 5–7, 17, 19, 33, 77, 104, 112, 116, 152, 161, 179–80, 183, 200, 203, 208, 210
stock market 27, 111–12, 175

T

taxation 76, 119, 124, 148, 185, 188, 193, 224
Temasek 41–3, 47
threats 99, 103, 146
transactions 14–15, 21, 51, 54, 95, 127–9, 133–5, 173–5, 178, 191
transparency 4–5, 9–10, 37–41, 44, 57–9, 67, 88, 91, 107, 110–12, 139, 150–8, 184, 210

V

violations 134, 138, 172–3, 191–2
voting 26, 87, 117, 120–2, 150–1, 160–3, 171–2, 185–7, 219

W

women, representation of 202, 217–36
workshops 27, 198–201, 207–9